THE MONTH OF MARY

The Annunciation
— Joos van Cleve, 1525

Month of Mary

OR

PRACTICAL MEDITATIONS FOR EACH DAY OF
THE MONTH OF MAY

BY THE

ABBÉ BERLIOUX

Translated from the tenth French edition by

LÆTITIA SELWYN OLIVER

With Preface By
THE MOST REV. DR. HEDLEY
Bishop of Newport and Menevia

MEDIATRIX PRESS
MMXXII

ISBN: 978-1-957066-25-7

Nihil Obstat:
P. J. TYNAN, S.T.D.,
Cens. Theol. Dep.

Imprimatur:
✠ Eduardus Card. Mac Cabe,
   ARCHIEPISCOPUS DUBLINENSIS.

Imprimatur :
✠ GULIELMUS
ARCHIEPISCOPUS DUBLINENSIS,
HIBERNIÆ PRIMAS.

Mediatrix Press
607 E 6th Ave
Post Falls, ID 83854
www.mediatrixpress.com

CONTENTS

PREFACE

THE little work of which this is a translation has already run through twelve editions in France. The writer, a parish priest of Grenoble, has been honored with a letter of approval and benediction from the late Pontiff;[1] and several of the French bishops, besides the Bishop of Grenoble, have examined and recommended the book.

There seems no historical record of the beginning of the devotion now so widely spread under the name of the "Month of Mary." It is certain that it took its origin in Italy, probably in Rome itself; and anyone who has been in Rome in May, and seen the wealth and profusion of sweet and lovely flowers which pour in from the country into the markets and streets of the city will think it very natural that the shrines and altars of the Madonna should be specially honored with fresh flowers at the moment when nature is so bountiful. There is a line of Latin verse which is said to exist still (we cannot vouch for the fact) on the capital of

---

[1] Pius IX.

a pillar in the old Abbey Church of Cluny. The Virgin Mother stands in the midst of an aureola of glory, round which run the words:— *"Ver primos flores, primos adducit honores"*—the spring-tide brings the first flowers, first to honor Mary. Pope Pius VI, in 1815, granted an indulgence of 300 days, for each day, to all who shall honor the Blessed Virgin during the month of May with prayer or other devotion; and a plenary indulgence once in the month to all who keep up this devotion every day in the month. Since then this devout practice has spread over the greater part of Europe.

The conditions under which holy religion at present exists in these countries make the cultivation of devotion to the holy Mother of God especially difficult. On the one hand, all enlightened spiritual men tell us (and there can be no doubt about it), that intimate, continuous, and tender devotion to Mary is essential both for personal holiness and for effecting conversions. On the other, the mental and spiritual state of our fellow-countrymen almost necessitates in regard to the prerogatives and cultus of the Blessed Virgin a sort of "discipline of the secret." I think we can hardly question this. First of all, there are many who have to be made to believe in God and immortality, and with whom the honor of God's

Mother is as unpractical a thought as that of the history of life in the farthest planet. Next, there are the cultivated non-Catholics of the country who languidly believe in God and attend Church on Sunday, and these, hardly knowing what worship is or heartfelt prayer, cannot even take in the conditions of the question of Mary's place in God's counsels. And lastly, there are the widespread ranks of dissent, where the "Romish" superstition is coarsely defined by the three words Popery, the worship of the Virgin, and sacerdotalism, and where the name of Mary, heard in a sermon or read in a book, simply causes a rancorous repulsion. Now, it is an elementary point of faith and practice that when things Catholic provoke the unbeliever to "blaspheme," they must be kept away from him, always provided there is no command or circumstance of charity or justice which directs otherwise. And it may be safely said that to bring the ordinary non-Catholic, without preparation, face to face with most holy Mary—with her rosary and her scapular, with the abandon and childlike excesses of Italian practices, with the expression of certain most true doctrines founded on her nearness to Jesus—is to do what is sure, unless by a miracle, to repel him and not to attract. A miracle we have no right to expect. And this is one of the troubles which preachers and priests generally have to face. Their own people naturally both understand the Mother of God, and long to hear her highest praises and to devote themselves to her in the most Catholic fashion. But there are Protestants in the Church! The good priest must either enter into cold explanations, or he must run the risk of driving away the inquirer with the conviction that the Roman Catholics worship Mary instead of Jesus.

This is a real trouble, and the result, as far as Protestants are concerned, is by no means imaginary. It is hardly a sufficient answer to say that we should fearlessly exhibit the most full and fervent Catholic spirit and leave the results to God. This proposition is most true, but it raises many sub-questions; and the simple fact is that the Church, in dealing with unbelievers, has always exercised reserve. But at the same time I am most decidedly of opinion that very little is ever really lost by the most explicit and uncompromising exaltation of the Mother of God, provided a little caution (not by any means coldness or minimizing cowardice) be shown, whether in sermons or in practices.

For we must remember that, in ordinary circumstances at least, our first duty is to our own people. They have a right to hear Mary spoken of as she really is. They have been brought up to love her most sweet name, and she is a part of their very innermost spiritual life. Or if they are converts, it has perhaps been this very attraction to the Mother of God which has had a large share in drawing them. To the flock, it is unjust that a preacher's words should have the warmth taken out of them because of the presence of Protestants. To the simple Catholic it is unjust that he should not be allowed to visit the Lady Altar as he likes, or kneel before the statue of the Immaculate, or follow Mary's effigy in procession, because there are some people present to whom those things may do harm. The Church must live her life, just as the earth must go round the sun; and things we regret do sometimes result from the one as from the other. And then, though we may not expect a miracle, yet the supernatural aspect of the matter must not be left out. Besides the direct advantages to the Catholic heart of devotion to the Blessed Virgin, it is certain that the indirect effect of the full Catholic worship and spirit upon non-Catholics must be very great. To work in God's way is always and inevitably to succeed; and there is much more chance of converting a Protestant country when priests and people understand the Mother of Jesus and work fervently up to the very limits of what they understand, than if their fears, even their prudent fears, keep them more silent and more sober. Their very courage and spirit of confessorship will draw down God's blessing; for courage is often required, in these countries, to live up to one's knowledge of Mary. When prelates and priests with a name in literary and scientific circles, or laymen who by no means relish being set down as superstitious, calmly let themselves be known as childlike clients of the Blessed Mother of our Lord, it is a very natural impulse which possesses them to want to explain the thing clearly to non-believing spectators. And although I have said that Protestants are sometimes repelled by being brought without preparation into the presence of Catholic devotion, yet it may happen that they are not repelled; and then the feeling of the actuality and reality of what they witness is sure to have a powerful effect in their convictions. Allowing for all the imperfections which accompany human action, still the life of the Church is a divine life, and its force, its truth, its naturalness, and its consistency must affect the unprejudiced mind or heart as the daylight affects the eye. Whatever the Church ordains or approves, whatever the saints have written, has a power of its own which it is wrong not to reckon upon. There is an interesting illustration of this in Professor Ornsby's admirable life of the late Mr. Hope-Scott.[2] In a letter from Rome, Mr. Hope-Scott, who was still an Anglican, mentions how he made friends with an ancient brother-porter of the Trappists. "I hardly ever met a more affectionate creature. He came up to my room at night with Liguori's book upon the B.V.M., and exacted a promise from me that if ever I should become a R.C. I would write to tell him of my conversion." He adds that, although he was engaged in a good deal of controversy, this was the "shrewdest encounter" he ever had. There is no reason for surprise if it was, and the proceeding of the old lay-brother is an instance of a certain essentially Catholic method of controversy which may not be always in season, but which probably is out of season much less commonly than some good people suppose.

As for the "caution" that was spoken of just now, what is meant may, I think, be summed up in three rules:—First, with non-Catholics, begin at the foundation, and not in the middle or at the top. With some, one has to begin with the Church; with others one has to go back to Jesus Christ; and with

---

[2] Vol. I., p. 259.

others again to God and immortality. No much less words to describe; she is a universe where suns and systems roll and shine in depths of space far out of reach to mortal powers of sight or search. If we gaze, if we think, if we pray, if we love, words can never fail should the world last a million years. But if there be not thought and love, then as the glories of the heavens or the sea may be spoiled by ignorance, by vulgarity, by puerile conceits and declamation, so may the Mother of Jesus.

If charity, or the love and worship of God only, be the end and perfect work for which our hearts are divinely fashioned, and if devotion is the flower of charity, then is affectionate nearness to Mary the most precious of graces. With her we do not learn so much as feel what Jesus is and what God is. She is a spiritual universe. A great world of power, of gifts, and of perfections which sends up to the Heart of Jesus an endless song of praise and adoration; and to other hearts, to the hearts of us who are given to her, she is a universe of force, a world of transforming power, influencing mind and will, imagination and desire; the more we know her the more closely we press to her feet by the use of all the faculties which God has given us. She has the gift to draw men from the mists of error to the serenity of faith. She can lift men up and set all this world below their feet, to live for heaven alone. She can pierce with a celestial spear the very life of self-love and set the spirit free to be God's and God's alone. Her pure hands shed on weak men and women the magic essence gathered where the cross stood, which turns pain into heroic love; and it is her example, as some mighty note of music, which sets the divinely made human heart to vibrate with the same singing of loving worship as her own most sinless heart.

May this book spread still further the light of her life and the sound of her praise!

JOHN CUTHBERT HEDLEY, O.S.B.
Bishop of Newport and Menevia,

Cardiff, *Feast of the Annunciation, 1884.*

Month of Mary

OPENING OF THE MONTH OF MAY

THE EVE

I. Origin of the devotion of the Month of Mary.
II. Advantages and Practices of this devotion.

FIRST POINT.—One beautiful evening in May, towards the end of the last century, a peasant child in Rome gathered round him some little companions and led them to a statue of the Blessed Virgin, where, according to the custom of the Holy City, a lamp was kept burning, and their pure and simple voices sang the Litany of Our Lady. The day after this little band returned to the feet of the Madonna, followed by other children. Their mothers next joined the devout assembly, and afterwards other groups were formed, and the devotion soon became popular. Holy souls, grieving over the scandals which increase in number and gravity with the return of the joyous season of spring, saw in these practices a design of Providence, and they responded to it by favoring this new devotion as an act of public and solemn reparation.

Whilst the votaries of the world hastened to their villas fragrant with the perfume of the freshly opened flowers, fervent and devout souls offered at the feet of the Immaculate Virgin their prayers and supplications, and thus was the month of Mary founded.

Springing up in the Holy City, as an impulse of love, under the beautiful sky of Italy and the eyes of the Holy Father, this touching devotion soon entered France and spread to all parts of the Catholic world. It was the little grain of mustard seed which developed rapidly, and multiplied everywhere its flowers and fruits.

What an admirable institution is the month of Mary! It is the month of spring and of flowers! it belongs then to our beloved Mother, whom Holy Scripture calls the Flower of the Fields, the Lily of the Valleys, the Rose of the Gardens of Jericho. It is a dangerous month, also, on account of the pleasures which this bright spring time brings, but consecrated to Mary, it becomes for all a month of innocence and holiness.

Children of the best of Mothers, let us hail with joy the dawn of this blessed month, which brings us each year so much joy, happiness, and consolation. In the words of Scripture, "this month shall be to you the beginning of months, it shall be the first in the months of the year" (Exod. 12:2).

Second Point.—Let no one doubt but that the Blessed Virgin has special favors to distribute during this beautiful month consecrated to her. If a mother on her feast day knows not how to refuse any favor to her children when gathered around her, they vie with each other in their expressions of filial love, what may we not hope for from Mary, who is preeminently a mother, and whom we are going to invoke during this long feast of thirty days. Blessed days, in which graces are more abundant, when God is nearer to us, and the Queen of Heaven is more occupied with her children on earth, Mary, the Mother of God, is so powerful, she is so good, she is indeed our Mother. Opening wide our hearts let us increase our desires, the Blessed Virgin will fulfil them: *Dilata os tuum et implebo illud.*

The following are a few practices to help us to sanctify this beautiful month:

1. If we are able to do so, let us assist each day at the pious exercises of the month of May: Public prayer, the word of God, harmonious chants, the flowers and lights which deck the altar of the Blessed Virgin, all these raise the soul to her throne and excite devotion.

2. Let us hear Mass more frequently, especially on Saturday, which is, as it were, the Sunday of the Mother of God.

3. During the month let us approach once at least to Holy Communion. This mark of love to her Divine Son is most pleasing to our Holy Mother.

It is by such practices that we shall merit the protection of the Queen of Mercy, and that we shall gain the precious indulgences which are attached to the devotion of the month of May.

EXAMPLE

A missionary priest was once preaching a retreat to the Confraternity of "Christian Mothers" of Nancy, and in one of his sermons he reminded them that no one must ever despair of the salvation of any soul, and that sometimes actions of little importance in the eyes of men are rewarded by God in a particular manner at the hour of death. He had just left the church when a lady in deep mourning came up to him, and spoke in these words, "Father, you have just recommended hope and confidence; an incident which happened to myself corroborates your words. I had a husband,

4

good, affectionate, but without any religion. Neither my prayers nor the few words I ventured to address to him on the subject had any effect.

"During the month of May which preceded his death, I had erected a little altar to the Blessed Virgin in my room, and I kept it decorated with fresh flowers. Every Sunday my husband spent the day in the country; on his return during this month he offered me a nosegay which he had himself gathered, and I placed these flowers on the altar. I know not if my husband observed it, or whether he did this merely to give me pleasure, or if it was some feeling of devotion towards the Blessed Virgin that moved him to it. But this is certain, that he never missed a single Sunday, and I let no day pass without praying to Our Lady for him.

"At the beginning of the following month he was suddenly struck dead without having time to receive the last Sacraments. I was inconsolable, and my health being seriously affected, my family obliged me to go to the South of France. As I passed near Lyons I wished to see the holy Curé d'Ars. Hardly had I entered his presence, than he said, 'Madame, you are in great grief, but have you forgotten the nosegays of flowers each Sunday of the month of May?'

"It is impossible to describe my astonishment

5

on hearing M. Vianney recall to my memory a circumstance which I had never told to anyone, and which he could only know by revelation. He added, 'God, moved by your prayers has had pity on him, because he honored the Blessed Virgin; at the moment of death your husband repented. His soul is now in purgatory, and by our prayers and good works we will obtain his release.'"

This fact, published in the weekly paper of Cambray, should induce us to celebrate devoutly the beautiful month of Mary. The smallest sacrifices, the most simple prayers, will please our Mother, provided we make them with confidence, love, and perseverance.

PRAYER

O sweet Mother of our Savior, and our Mother also, behold us prostrate at thy feet, to offer thee the first-fruits of this beautiful month. We will bless and love thee, and imitate each day thy virtues. Vouchsafe to listen to our prayers and hymns, to receive our flowers, but above all accept the offering of our hearts, Oh, may we from this first hour, drawn by the odors of thy virtues, follow the saints on the path to heaven.

FIRST DAY

THE MEANS OF SPENDING THE MONTH OF MAY WORTHILY

I. We must love Mary with more tenderness.
II. We must pray to her with more fervor.

First Point.—"Let us love Mary," exclaims St. Bernard, "with all our hearts, with all the strength of our affections." Such is the will of God. By her He has given us his Son; by her He communicates to us all graces, *"Omnia per Mariam."* Let us love Mary. All the saints invite us to do so, by their example and by their words. What language could express all they said and did to honor and serve her? Let us love Mary. All the Doctors of the Church affirm, and experience teaches that a tender and generous love for the Mother of God is a certain sign of salvation. "If," said a great saint, "I have the happiness of loving the Blessed Virgin, with my whole heart, I am certain of perseverance; heaven is mine."

Children of Mary, recollect yourselves; ask your own hearts if its affections are consecrated to the Mother of God? If at this moment she addressed to you the same question which Jesus asked St. Peter, "Lovest thou me?" would you dare to reply, "Thou knowest, O my Mother, that I love thee." Alas! is not your heart filled by those creatures which you have loved so long, and which perhaps you still passionately love? The month of May was an inspiration of love. Endeavor then, during these happy days, to acquire a tender devotion and an ardent affection for our Heavenly Mother, by meditating each day on her privileges, her virtues, her goodness, and mercy. "O Mary! who would not love thee? Thou art more beautiful than the sun, sweeter than honey."[1] "I will not rest till I obtain a tender love for thee, my beloved Mother."[2]

Second Point.—Wishing to induce his religious to address their prayers with confidence to Mary, the devout St. Bernard said, "Brethren, go without fear to the Blessed Virgin, pray lovingly to her, you will always find her ready to grant you all you ask." This great saint was so convinced that the Queen of

---

[1] St. Bernard.

[2] Blessed Berchmans.

8

Heaven never refuses anything to those who invoke her with confidence, that he exclaimed, I consent, O most Holy Virgin, that he shall not speak of thy mercy who, having invoked thee, was not heard." The Church places in the mouth of this tender Mother these beautiful words: "Blessed is the man that heareth me, and that watcheth daily at my gates." (Prov. 8:34.) If one single prayer is like an arrow which, piercing her heart, opens thereby a stream of mercy, will not the prayers of an entire month draw down floods of benedictions and graces?

Children of the best of Mothers, let not this favorable occasion pass. During this month consecrated to her, ask her for all the graces that you stand in need of. Pray to her for yourself, for your family, for the head of the Church, for your country, for poor sinners, for the souls in purgatory. If hitherto your prayers to Mary have been few and cold, let them this month be more frequent and fervent. Oh, yes, pray often, ask much, and ask with confidence, then will all your requests be granted. "Heaven and earth shall pass away," says Louis de Blois "sooner than the Blessed Virgin should fail to assist those who have recourse to her."

EXAMPLE

A French colonel who was seriously wounded at the siege of Sebastopol, had a sister of Bon Secours to nurse and attend him. "Sister," said the invalid, "I am a Protestant, and such I shall remain until death, so do not speak to me of religion; attend only to your duties as nurse." The sister did as she was bid. At first she said her prayers before him, but seeing that it excited the sneers of the colonel, and caused him to say impious things, she left off praying in his presence and continued to be very gentle and watchful over him. The colonel was touched by this act of delicacy, and after a time told the sister that she might say her prayers—he even felt that they did him good.

"Sister," said he one day, "you were praying just now, and you looked compassionately at me: why did you do so?"

The sister replied, "Oh, sir, I will not conceal the fact: it was for you that I was praying, for you, my brother in Jesus Christ, who are on the brink of hell. I asked Mary, the refuge of sinners, to have pity on you: I wished to influence the Son through the Mother."

"But, sister, I am a Protestant."

"I know it," replied the sister; "you do not invoke the Blessed Virgin, but she will have pity on you, for she is your Mother."

"Well, then, sister, continue your prayers to the Blessed Virgin," said the colonel, "for they do me good." From that moment the invalid was no longer the same man, his heart was touched, and his eyes were opened to the light of faith. A priest was brought to him, who instructed him, heard his confession, and reconciled him to God. Death was near at hand, the invalid awaited it calmly, but he had yet something to do. He sent for a number of the officers of his regiment, and asked pardon for all the scandals he had given them, declaring that he died a child of the Catholic Church. A few days after this event, he calmly expired whilst the sister, kneeling at his bedside, was recommending his soul to God. Oh, wonderful effect of prayer! Oh, goodness of Mary, which is never invoked in vain!

PRAYER

O Mary, my Sovereign, I am unworthy to appear in thy presence, but nevertheless I will invoke thee each day of this blessed month. My tender Mother, when I come to thee in prayer, cast on me a look of compassion; when I offer thee a sacrifice, give me thy blessing; when I make an act of love, speak to my heart. From this day forward I give thee my heart, entirely and without reserve: it belongs to thee, keep it always, and let it repose on thine. Amen.

SECOND DAY

THE IMMACULATE CONCEPTION

I. The glory which this privilege procures to Mary.
II. The confidence with which it should inspire us.

First Point.—Let us admire the glory which the title of Immaculate Conception procures to Mary. It is a singular glory. All men are born children of wrath, slaves of the devil, and no longer heirs of heaven. But, oh, wonderful sight, in the midst of this universal ruin, one creature stands alone, and this privileged creature is the Blessed Virgin, who rises as a lily without spot in the midst of thorns. Hers is an unchangeable glory. All in her is holy and perfect; she was resplendent in sanctity at her birth, during her life, at death, and, says St. Epiphanius, she will ever be without sin and without fault. Hers is an incomprehensible glory. Mary received at her conception graces so wonderful and so extraordinary, that even then, in the language of the Fathers, she was a world of magnificence and the wonder of creation. And, what most of all brings joy to her heart, is not her title of Queen of

Heaven, nor that of Sovereign of the world, but of her Immaculate Conception. O Mother of God! my Mother also, how great is thy glory, how it fills me with gladness, and what happiness it gives me to say to thee with the Universal Church, "Thou art all fair, and there is no spot in thee."

By holy baptism, which the Fathers of the Church call the Sacrament of our Spiritual Conception, our souls have been purified from the stain of original sin, and we have been raised to the dignity of children of God. But how long have we preserved pure and spotless the beautiful robe of our baptismal innocence? Alas, how often have we stained it by the filth of mortal sin? Oh! if at this hour we are still in this lamentable state, let us hasten to purify our souls by a good confession, and for the future let us take as our motto: "Death sooner than stain." — *Potius mori quam fædari.*

Second Point.—If this privilege is glorious for our Mother it is not less advantageous to us her children. She is always disposed to hear those who honor her under this title. Mary conceived without sin, has been invoked by tempted souls, and they have triumphed over the temptation; by afflicted souls, and they have been consoled; by troubled hearts, and they have found peace; by weak hearts ready to fail, and they have been strengthened. The inhabitants of besieged towns have inscribed on their doors, "Mary was conceived without sin," and they have been preserved; houses on fire, persons in peril of death, have been saved by writing or by saying the same words. The medal of Mary conceived without sin, has filled the world with wonders, it has averted misfortunes, drawn down graces, converted sinners and merited to be proclaimed everywhere, as the miraculous medal. Finally, the Blessed Virgin vouchsafed to appear at Lourdes, saying: "I am the Immaculate Conception," and since then, she showers her most signal favors on those who invoke her under this title and make this ever celebrated pilgrimage. Does it need more to prove that the mystery of the Immaculate Conception is a treasure of grace in which we should have entire confidence?

Children of Mary, often and confidently invoke Mary Immaculate. In times of weakness and depression, in your afflictions and in your dangers, raise your eyes to this sweet Queen, say to her with faith and love: "O Mary conceived without sin, pray for us," and joy, peace, strength, and hope, will revive in your hearts. O Immaculate Queen! remember your children, intercede for them, and save them from sin and eternal death. Queen, conceived without original sin, pray for us. *Regina sine labe concepta, ora pro nobis.*

EXAMPLE

A young man who had been a model of piety up to the age of twenty-one was the comfort of his widowed mother. From his childhood he had worn the scapular of the Immaculate Conception, and repeated night and morning the invocation, "O Mary, conceived without sin." Influenced by two worldly friends, he gradually gave himself up to a life of dissipation. He left his mother, and led such a wild life, that worn out, whilst still young, he three years later fell dangerously ill of consumption. He was living at the time in a country-house near Geneva. His pious mother went to him, and forgetting the past, nursed him with the tender care that only a mother can show. She spoke to him gently of the necessity of being reconciled to God, and the poor Prodigal replied coldly: "Do not speak to me on that subject, it is useless; I have done too much, I have gone too far;" and on two occasions he rudely refused to see a priest. All seemed lost, when his mother was inspired to remind him of his former love for the Immaculate Virgin, of his daily prayer and scapular, and kneeling near his bed, she persuaded him to say with her the invocation he had so often repeated, "O Mary, conceived without sin." He consented and prayed with his mother. At that moment his eyes filled with tears, his heart was softened. The work was done, the Blessed Virgin had saved her child. He asked for the priest whom he had dismissed, he made his confession, received Communion, and expired happily, invoking for the last time the Virgin conceived without sin. Thus is the Queen of Heaven pleased to bless those who invoke her under the title of her Immaculate Conception.

PRAYER

Immaculate Virgin, more holy than St. John the Baptist, who was sanctified in his mother's womb, more pure than the angels who call thee their Queen, help us to overcome the terrible consequences of original sin. Alas! what struggles, what combats have we not to endure. Oh! thou who wert conceived and who always lived without sin, pray for us sinners, who with confidence have recourse to thee.

THIRD DAY

THE HOLY NAME OF MARY

I. A name of Power.
II. A name of Sweetness.

First Point.—We may in a certain sense apply to the name of Mary, what St. Paul says of the adorable name of Jesus, that it is all-powerful in heaven, on earth, and in hell. In heaven the name of Mary, emanating from the treasures of the Divinity, is loved by the Father, the Son, and the Holy Spirit, who cannot hear it without being moved. The angels and the saints bow respectfully at the name of Mary, and are ever ready to obey at the first sign of her will. On earth nothing can withstand those who call upon her with confidence and love. St. Anselm says that there are times when the invocation of the name of Mary obtains help more speedily than the invocation of the name of Jesus. Lastly, it is a power truly invincible against the infernal hosts, and the Church has always triumphed through the invocation of this name. Each time that the serpent, trying to withdraw his head from under the crushing foot of the Virgin, has, endeavored to spread over the world the poison of falsehood and error, the Church has invoked the all-powerful name of Mary Immaculate, and heresies have been destroyed.

Oh, you who are justly proud of the title of Children of Mary, make it your happiness to repeat often her sacred name. It will be your shield in the battle of salvation, your strength in temptations, your protection in perils, your light in your doubts, your support in life, and your hope at the hour of death. Oh! holy Mary, I ask of thee but one grace; grant that thy name may be always present to the memory of thy servant: shielded by this powerful protection, I shall be certain not to perish.

Second Point.—The name of Mary is indeed a name indescribably harmonious, it is a name of sweetness, a name which refreshes the soul and fills the heart with fragrance. "It falls more soothingly on the ear," says a saint, "than the most charming melody, it is sweeter to the mouth than the honeycomb, it rejoices the heart more than the purest joy." Mary is the name lisped by the child at its mother's knee, sung by the young girl in her hymns, uttered hopefully by the afflicted in their misery, repeated constantly by the orphan in his misfortunes, invoked by the sinner upon his repentance, and breathed by the dying on their couch of pain. Mary! Mary! it is the name which in ecstasies of joy is sung in heaven on harps of gold, and the whole earth re-echoes the sound. Mary is the name of a Mother, of the Mother of Jesus, of our Mother, and love is never weary of repeating it. Who would refuse to invoke unceasingly or to bless this sacred name, which has dried so many tears and never caused one to flow. O Jesus! O Mary! may your holy names be always in my heart and often on my lips!

Remember, Children of Mary, that the name which was given you on the day of your baptism, is taken from the catalogue of the saints, and secures for you a special patron in heaven. Bear this name with honor and dignity, like the blessed soul, who ennobled it by its battles on earth, and who glorifies it eternally in heaven by its triumphs. Have a particular devotion towards your holy patron; read his life, imitate his virtues, pray to him daily, and celebrate his yearly feast with piety. Oh! great saint, whose name I am privileged to bear, pray for me and protect me always in life and in death.

EXAMPLE

In one of the countries of Asia, a little child was taught at school to sing the Hail Mary, and he loved to recite it on his knees before an image of the Blessed Virgin. He found such sweetness in this prayer that he went about reciting it in the streets. Each time he pronounced the name of Mary his face became animated, his eyes were lifted towards heaven, and his voice was more melodious. In the town there were scoffers who detested the little minstrel of the Mother of God. One day he was stopped by an assassin, who nearly murdered him, and threw his body into a ditch. The poor weeping mother went about seeking her son, and God conducted her to the ditch.

Oh! wonderful miracle, the dying child still murmured the name of Mary, "Maria," but with so sweet a voice, it seemed as if it came from heaven. He was carried to the nearest church, and the priest asked the child how it was that he could sing.

"When I was about to die," replied the young martyr, "the holy Virgin said to me, 'Once more sing my praises, repeat at least my name; soon I will come and seek you, and lead you to the temple of my Son.'"

Pronouncing once again the name of Mary, "Maria," he fell asleep in the Lord, The poor mother was filled with consolation, seeing that her son was happy in heaven. Happy, indeed, shall we too be if we find in the sweet name of Mary the same attraction and the same charm. Oh! if we could die with the names of Jesus and Mary on our lips. "Blessed and precious," says St. Liguori, "the death which is protected by these saving names."

PRAYER

O holy Virgin, how sweet and powerful is thy name. It opens heaven and closes hell, it chains fast the devil, it fills the heart with fragrance. Oh! how many dangers should I have avoided, how many falls should I have escaped, how many victories should I have gained, what happiness should I have enjoyed, if I had always had recourse to thy sacred name and to the name of Jesus. Henceforth I will invoke it in my dangers, it shall be my strength and my consolation during the remaining days of my life and at the hour of my death. Amen.

FOURTH DAY

MARY, MOTHER OF GOD

I. To what high dignity Mary is raised by this title.
II. How deeply she abases herself by her humility.

First Point.—St. Thomas and St. Bonaventure find
nothing to which to compare the title of Mother of
God, which belongs to Mary, to the exclusion of
every other creature. God alone is supremely good,
but the Blessed Virgin comes the nearest to the
divine perfections; she borders upon the Infinite.
"Listen, O man," exclaims St. Anselm, "contemplate
and admire! The eternal Father had an only and
consubstantial Son, but He did not will that this
Son should belong to Him alone, He gave Him to
Mary, and she is really his Mother on earth, as God
is his Father in heaven. What a marvel, and who
but God Himself could work such a miracle.
Virginity and fruitfulness are united, and a virgin
conceived in time that same Son whom God had
begotten from all eternity. Who, before Mary, had
ever heard of so great a wonder? A mother had

23

exclaimed in former ages when showing her children: 'Behold my glory, behold my crown.' Yet the renown which those children had acquired was but the echo of the little fame they had gained in the world. But the child whom Mary shows us, and whom she can with justice call her glory and her crown, is the true Son of God, the Savior of men. To what a height of dignity and glory is a mere creature raised."

Nevertheless, Children of Mary, we need not envy the happiness of the Mother of Jesus, since by Holy Communion we ourselves become partakers of it. Indeed, the Eucharist is an extension of the Divine mystery of the Incarnation, and each one of us, after Communion, can exclaim, "My God is mine; I possess Him, and God, all-powerful as He is, can give me nothing greater than Himself. May my soul forever bless Him. My soul doth magnify the Lord." From henceforth let us look on Holy Communion as the highest honor to which we can aspire, and let us often approach the Eucharistic Banquet. St. Gertrude assures us that she would have passed over swords in order to go to the Holy Table. O Mary! make my eagerness like to hers, at least on thy greatest festivals.

Second Point.—"Oh, marvel of humility!" exclaims

St. Bernard, "the higher Mary is raised the more deeply she abases herself." The Archangel Gabriel bends before her, and saluting her as full of grace, announces that the Most Holy Trinity has chosen her to be the Mother of the Messiah. The humble virgin of Juda was troubled, and could not understand how the choice of God could fall on her lowliness. The angel displayed before her eyes the magnificence of the divine maternity, and the greatness of the Son she was about to bring forth; but this only made her shrink from so high a dignity; she thought of the humiliations of the Incarnate Word, and she humbled herself and was confounded at her own nothingness. To all the praises bestowed upon her she had but one answer, and it well expresses the sentiments which animated her: "Behold the handmaid of the Lord."—*Ecce ancilla Domini*. "You speak to me of being his Mother, I am but his handmaid;" and not content with believing that she is nothing in herself, she wishes all to be persuaded of her nothingness, so that all praise and glory may be given to God alone, Thus in her sublime Canticle, called by St. Ambrose the Ecstasy of Humility, she repeats to all ages that God hath regarded the humility of his handmaid, and that all generations shall call her blessed. Oh, marvel of humility!

delighting heaven and inducing the Son of God to descend from his throne of glory to the abyss of our nothingness. *Humilitate concepit.*

Children of Mary, may the example of our Mother convince us that humility is the source of all graces and the best disposition for receiving the Holy Eucharist. To be "vessels of election" fitted to receive Jesus in the Blessed Sacrament, we must at least, says St. Augustine, be void of self. God withdraws from the proud, but He gives Himself to the humble. O Jesus! O Mary! grant that each Communion may find in us some sentiments of humility similar to those which animated you at the moment of the Incarnation.

EXAMPLE

When in exile in Brussels, General Lamoricière had the happiness to return to God, and from that moment he made rapid progress in virtue and piety. He had three books which he constantly made use of, a catechism, a missal, and an Imitation of Christ. One day when in Paris he joined in a discussion, before one of his daughters, with the priest of the parish, on frequent Communion. "We are not worthy to communicate so often," said he.

"It is true," replied the priest; "but we stand in need of it. Communion is not so much a reward as a grace and a help. Unworthy of so great a favor, we ought to humble ourselves like the Blessed Virgin, at the moment of the Incarnation: *humilitate concepit.* Poor and destitute as we are of everything, we should often have recourse to the Holy Eucharist, for it is the source of all good."

The General paused a moment, and then said: "Rev. Father, hitherto many unsatisfactory reasons have been given me, but you now give me a good one, and I thank you for it." Then turning to his daughter he said: "This is quite enough, my child; go to Communion as often as you can, but let it be with feelings of deep humility." Frequently did the illustrious General accompany his pious daughter to the Eucharistic Banquet, and many times did the warrior, who had faced death unmoved on the battle-field, shed tears when receiving the God of armies. When asked on his death-bed if he wished to receive Communion for the last time, he replied, with lively faith, "Oh, yes, I ardently desire it, all unworthy though I am!" And, after having communicated, he happily expired in the arms of his daughter, pronouncing the sweet names of Jesus, Mary, and Joseph. Let us also, Children of

Mary, communicate as often as we can, but always with a lively faith and profound humility.

PRAYER

O Mary, thou who didst humble thyself so much the more deeply the higher thou wert raised by God, obtain for us, thy children, thy own spirit of humility. Alas! we are but little inclined to imitate thee; we seek only what may feed our pride and flatter our self-love. Cast upon us one look of mercy, and teach us to be meek and humble of heart. Amen.

FIFTH DAY

MARY IS OUR MOTHER

I. By her love.
II. By her sorrows.

First Point.—At what moment of her life did the Blessed Virgin make that ineffable act of love which gave her to us as our mother? It was at that solemn moment when the Archangel Gabriel announced to her the great mystery of the Incarnation. But in revealing to her that she was to be raised to the dignity of Mother of God, may he not have made known to her all the sorrows that would be hers in consequence of her divine maternity. She may have seen in prophetic vision God Incarnate ascending Calvary, dying on the cross, and confiding all Christians to the keeping of her love. Did Mary consent to this martyrdom, which was to end only with her life? All depended on her consent. "O compassionate Virgin!" exclaims St. Bernard, "have pity on us; dost thou not see the poor exiled Adam and Eve, our first mother, in tears, and the patriarchs, and the prophets, who implore thee, and all ages of the world prostrate at thy feet. O merciful arbitress of our destiny, say the word which is to save us!" Glory be to God, love to Mary, peace to earth! The august Virgin has spoken; she has given her loving consent; she has pronounced that word which makes her the mother of men; "Be it done unto me according to thy word."—*Fiat mihi secundum verbum tuum.* "I know that in becoming the Mother of God, I shall be also the Mother of Sorrows; nevertheless, I willingly consent for the salvation of my new children, my love shall be 'stronger than death.'" Be it done. *Fiat mihi.* The holy Fathers have extolled this admirable word of Mary, that "Fiat" so sweet and so great, which was really the creation of a new world, and the illustrious St. Bernard does not hesitate to say, that at the moment when the Virgin of Judea gave her decisive consent, she already carried us in her heart, as a mother carries her children.

Children of Mary, if we thought oftener of the immense love of Mary for us, how much more should we love her? How should we avoid everything that could displease her? Love is repaid only by love, and the child who loves not its mother is accursed by heaven. Let us, therefore, love Mary; the more we love her, the more she will love us. *Diligentes me diligo.* "O Mary, who delightest all hearts, why have you not long since captivated mine? "It belongs," says St. Bernard, "to thee; it loves thee."

Second Point.—But when and how did the Queen of Angels become our mother by sorrow? It was on Calvary, at the moment when Jesus, expiring on the cross, said to her: "Woman, behold thy son;" and to St. John, "Behold thy Mother." The Fathers of the Church are agreed that in St. John all the elect were represented. It was as if Jesus had said to Mary, "I am dying, but I leave you other children; you shall love not only the disciple who replaces me, but all mankind for whom I die. They shall be henceforth the object of your maternal solicitude. *Ecce filius tuus*: Behold thy son." And the boundless love of Mary received into her heart the whole human race. But this new maternity was an additional sorrow, and she had to undergo as much anguish in bringing forth mankind to their new life as she had joy in giving birth to her God. Oh! who can understand the grief of her heart when separated from Jesus. Who can even tell what she endured for us on the day of that great sacrifice? "My son," cries out Tobias, "thou shalt honor thy mother all the days of thy life, and forget not the pains thou hast caused her." Christians, children of tears and of sorrows, remember always the love and anguish of your Mother. The holy Curé d'Ars often said, with deep emotion, "that a good son should not be able to look at his mother without weeping." Woe to us if our hearts are unmoved at the sight of Mary at the foot of the cross, bringing us forth in tears. Oh! what an excess of love and what a true martyrdom.

EXAMPLE

After the massacre of Thessalonica it was decreed, that from each family of this important town one victim should be delivered up to justice. At the moment when the slaughter commenced there stood in the Amphitheater a man with his two sons, the one a strong youth, the hope of an illustrious house, the other still a child, and most tenderly loved. The soldier, or rather the executioner, asked the father which of these two he was to kill. The unhappy man gazed on his children and wept. "Choose," repeated the soldier; but choice was impossible. Taking them in his arms and pressing them to his heart, the father begged that one blow might kill them both. They fell, but only one had received the death stroke; and when from the stupor of sorrow the father returned to consciousness, the body of his eldest son lay weltering in its blood, whilst the youngest child clung weeping to his father's hand. On Calvary Divine Justice demanded a victim and God told Mary to choose between Jesus, her first born Son, and her other child, guilty man, and she made the choice; she consented to the death of Jesus, in order to secure life for us. Behold how she loved us! *Sic Maria dilexit.* See at what cost she has become our Mother. *Ecce Mater tua.*—Behold thy Mother. Oh! how ungrateful and guilty shall we be if we do not love a Mother so good and so devoted.

PRAYER

Remember, O holy Virgin, that we are the children of thy love and thy sorrow. Remember that we were bequeathed to thee by Jesus when dying on the cross, and that it was to thy tenderness and mercy that we were confided. Stretch forth thy hand, protect us now, and, above all, at the hour of death.

SIXTH DAY

MARY IS OUR MOTHER
(continued)

I. A powerful Mother.
II. A tender Mother.

First Point.—By her intimate connection with the Three Divine Persons the Blessed Virgin exercises immense power. She is the *Daughter of the Father.* He has chosen her to be the Mother of his Divine Son. "How great, then, must be her influence," says Bossuet, being thus associated with the Almighty power of God in the great work of our salvation." She ever finds favor in his sight. She is the Spouse of the Holy Spirit. Was it ever known that the request of a tenderly loved wife was rejected by her husband? Their two independent wills practically form but one, for what one asks is invariably granted by the other. What, then, will not Mary obtain from her heavenly Spouse, who regards her with so much favor, and from whom she has received the most sublime prerogatives? She is the *Mother of Jesus.* By this title she possesses incontestable rights and real authority over the Heart of her Divine Son. St. Peter Damian writes, that her prayers are orders rather than petitions. "*Non orans, sed imperans.*" "Ask what thou wilt, O my Mother," says Jesus. "All shall be granted to thee, for a Son can never refuse anything to a Mother whom He loves more than Himself." "*Non fas matrem refici.*"

Such is then the immensity of the power of the Blessed Virgin with the Holy Trinity as Daughter, Spouse, and Mother. Children of Mary, meditate well these three titles, and you will form an idea, which words cannot express, of the power of your Queen. See how marvelous are the effects of her influence; how many sick owe to her their health? how many poor the relief of their miseries? how many spiritually blind the light of faith?

"It would be impossible," says a pious writer, "to enumerate all the miracles of grace obtained through the powerful intercession of Mary; easier would it be to count the stars of heaven than the numbers of souls which she has saved from eternal perdition, and snatched from the tyranny of the devil." I acknowledge, O my Sovereign, that thy power is limitless and incomprehensible. Vouchsafe to use it in my behalf with thy Divine Son, and my salvation will be secured. *Virgo potens, ora pro nobis.*—Virgin most powerful, pray for us.

Second Point.—"But of what use," says St. Augustine, "would be Mary's great power, if she did not employ it in our favor? Oh! let us rejoice," adds this great Doctor of the Church; "for if she is the most powerful of creatures with God, she is also the most eager to come to our assistance. She can say, with greater truth than Job: 'From my infancy mercy grew up with me.'" Wishing to describe the mercy of Mary, St. Bernard writes thus: "O sublime Virgin, who can measure the length, the breadth, the height, or the depth of thy mercy? Its breadth fills the whole earth, its length extends to the end of time, its height reaches heaven, its depth penetrates even to purgatory. Behold," says he, "the reason of my great confidence in Mary. She has both the power to help me, being the Mother of the All-powerful, and the will to do so, for she is the Mother of Mercy."

Happy Children of Mary! would that I could make you understand how good a Mother Jesus has given you! Would that I could recount to you all her tenderness, all her sweetness, all her love for us! Tertullian once exclaimed: "There is no father like God." *Nemo tam Pater.* And we may add there is no mother like Mary, there is no heart like her heart. Oh, let us pity those who do not know her, or love her. Let us compassionate above all those separated from us in faith, those poor orphans of the Protestant church. *They* have no mother. And who will plead their cause in their day of need? Let us at least put no bounds to our confidence. Mary is our Mother. She loves us; she will never let us perish.

EXAMPLE

During the dreadful war of 1870 a woman came to one of the ambulances; she was dressed in mourning, and looked pale and sad. She carried a large parcel, which she placed on a table. A Sister of Charity seeing her, drew near. "Sister," said the stranger, "here is some linen and some provisions which I beg you to accept for your ambulance."

The sister thanked her, and as the stranger was about to leave, said: "Will you give me your name, madame?"

"Of what use will that be, sister?"

"I have to register the names of benefactors." replied the sister.

"Of what use will that be?" repeated the

stranger. Then suddenly changing her mind, she said, sadly and tearfully: "My name is of no importance; simply inscribe on your register 'a mother.' What I have brought you today I was keeping in reserve, in case my son, who belonged to one of the regiments of the guards, should be ill or wounded. Alas! the Prussians killed him at Champigny. I have now no use for these things; I had but one son, and he is dead. My name can interest no one. Accept these things for your wounded soldiers, and inscribe me as 'a mother.'" And the poor lady left the ambulance, followed by the Sister of Charity, who could not restrain her tears.

Oh! how true it is that the heart of a mother is the masterpiece of heaven, and how true it is also that there is in the heart of Mary more tenderness, more love, and more devotedness than in the united hearts of all earthly mothers. Let us then love her; she is our Mother; that word expresses all.

PRAYER

Yes, O Mary, thou art the Mother of love, thy goodness equals thy power, and thy maternal heart is always open to thy children. O be ever our good Mother, the Mother of those who labor, and of

those who weep, the Mother of just souls and of
poor sinners, the Mother of the young and of the
dying, the Mother of our country and of the
Church. Amen.

SEVENTH DAY

MARY IS OUR ADVOCATE

I. During life.
II. At death.

First Point.—"In Jesus Christ," says St. Paul, "we have an all-powerful advocate with the Father." "*Advocatum habemus apud Patrem.*" But in Mary we have also a most powerful advocate with the Son.—*Advocata nostra.* He Himself gave her this office, when from the cross He gave her to us to be our Mother. A mother, indeed, has not only the right but it is her duty to defend her children; and Mary, to use the beautiful words of St. Germanus, "is never weary of defending us." She pleads with the Son, and the Son, won to our side, pleads with the Father. She shows to Jesus her maternal bosom, and Jesus shows to his Father his open side and pierced hands. "During all ages she intercedes for mankind," say the Doctors of the Church, and standing ever near the throne of God, she pleads for the just and for sinners. A most charitable advocate, she invites us to place in her hands all our rights and all our interests. As a universal advocate she rejects no one, she receives all cases. As an eloquent and skillful advocate, she has never allowed any poor criminal for whom she pleaded to be condemned. "Oh, ineffable mercy of God," says a holy author, "who fearing to cast us from Him by a sentence of condemnation, has given us for our advocate his own Mother, the Queen of grace."

Children of Mary, say often to her, with St. Bernard "O Mother! thou who art our advocate, fulfil thy duties, speak in our favor; beg for us fervor and perseverance, and thou wilt be heard." "*Officium tuum imple.*" And you, above all, poor sinners, who stand most in need of her help, place your wants in her hands. The more desperate and hopeless your cause, the more interest and care will she give to it, and you will be saved. "Behold," says St. Anselm, "what grounds for hope it is the Divine Will to give you, since your salvation depends on Jesus Christ, your Brother, and Mary, your Mother. Jesus is both your Judge and your Advocate; Mary is both your advocate and your Mother. How sweet and consoling is this thought! Oh, sinners, poor sinners, open your hearts to confidence." "*O peccator ne diffidas!*"

Second Point.—If during life Mary holds the place of second mediatrix, she becomes our only one at the hour of death. Then in a certain sense we may say that Jesus ceases to be an advocate, to become our Judge; Mary alone is left us to undertake the great cause of our salvation. Oh! how great will be our need of this powerful advocate, in that hour of our last combat, on which depends our eternity. On one side a severe Judge, who will demand a rigorous account of all the actions of our life; on the other, a merciless accuser, Satan, who redoubling his efforts, multiplies his snares and his temptations. But will it be only one accuser? St. Liguori assures us that in this last combat the devil will not be satisfied to attack us alone; he will summon to his aid innumerable legions of infernal spirits who are pledged to drag our souls down to hell. But, Children of Mary, let us take courage; she whom we have so often invoked under the title of advocate will be there, bending over our death-bed, like a mother over the cradle of her infant, to defend us by her power against the enemies of our salvation, "During life," said she to St. Gertrude, "I pledge myself to obtain all necessary graces for my servants, but at death I come to them in person. I undertake their defense with my Divine Son, and with one look I put to flight all the powers of hell."

Oh! what happiness will be ours, at our last hour, that terrible moment, when there is but one step between us and eternity, if we can have at our side our beloved Mother, the august Queen, in whom Almighty God has deigned to bestow upon us so merciful, so powerful an advocate. O Mary! be our defense during life, and at the hour of death, and after this our exile shown unto us the blessed fruit of thy womb, Jesus.

EXAMPLE

During the terrible wars between England and France, Edward III, having taken Calais, consented to spare the town, on condition that six of the principal citizens should come to his camp with cords round their necks, and offer themselves as victims to his anger. Six virtuous and devoted men consented to make the sacrifice of their lives for the safety of the unfortunate town. But before presenting themselves to the king, they implored as a last resource the intercession and mediation of his wife. Prostrate at her feet, their eyes filled with tears, they exclaimed: "Oh! good and powerful Queen, be our advocate with the victorious king, plead our cause, obtain pardon for our city and for ourselves. If you abandon us we shall perish, if you intercede for us our lives will be saved; for pity's sake speak for us, O beloved Queen.

Touched with compassion, the royal lady raised them from the ground, and comforting them promised to undertake their defense. At that moment the king entered, and casting on them a look of anger, he ordered them to be put to death at once. "Prince," exclaimed the queen, "if you have accounted me worthy to be associated with you in your victories, if I have a right to share in your triumphs, I assert these rights in order to save these virtuous men. I ask for their pardon as the reward of my services, and my request must be granted." "Madame," replied the king, "I can refuse nothing to so powerful and so devoted a spouse, your clients are spared." The prisoners uttered a cry of joy and called down blessings on their noble benefactress.

Our Queen is Mary, she is our Sovereign Advocate, who implores pardon for us during life and at the hour of death, and her Divine Son gladly yields to the supplications of His Mother to pardon all sinners. Alas! how often would divine vengeance have burst over our guilty heads, had not Mary appeased the anger of her Son, and averted the scourges of his justice?

PRAYER

O Mother of Mercy, since thou art our Advocate, assist us during life, and plead the all important cause of our salvation. Protect our poor souls at the moment of death, and disperse the formidable troop of demons ready to assail us. Lastly, at the dread judgment save us from eternal damnation; grant that we may enter into the glorious kingdom of thy Son and enjoy the inheritance of the children of God. Amen.

EIGHTH DAY

THE SACRED HEART OF MARY

I. The most perfect of hearts.
II. The most loving of hearts.

First Point.—Reflect, O Children of Mary, that if it is your duty to honor the Sacred Heart of Jesus, the center of all the affections and sentiments of the God Man, it is also proper to offer to the Heart of your Mother the homage of veneration and love. The Most Holy Trinity united in enriching this admirable Heart with the most excellent gifts and precious favors. The Father manifested His Almighty power in creating the heart of a Daughter, full of respect and fidelity towards her Creator. The Son created the Heart of a Mother in which he deigned to dwell as in his sanctuary during nine months, The Holy Spirit made it the Heart of a Spouse in which to celebrate His ineffable nuptials. Finally, Mary has powerfully contributed to enrich and adorn her heart with virtues and merits, by her faithful correspondence to grace, by the sanctity and innocence of her life, and by the constant practice of every virtue. O God! who can ever fully understand the greatness, the treasures, the perfections enclosed in this vessel of singular devotion. It is a tabernacle full of sanctity which no impure breath has ever tarnished; it is a garden adorned and strictly enclosed, into which no human passions have ever penetrated. In a word, it is a Heart above all hearts, incomparable and perfect. *"Una est columba mea, perfecta mea."* —"One is my dove, my perfect one" (Cant. 6:8). Figure to yourselves the angels descending from heaven to earth in order to honor this Immaculate Heart, which contains within itself all the perfections which the blessed inhabitants of the Celestial City possess in different degrees.

Ah! if we but enter into ourselves, if we but compare our hearts with that of Mary our model, now imperfect, how poor and wretched will they not appear. Vessels sanctified by baptism, and the Body and Blood of Jesus Christ, they have become by sin whitened sepulchers full of dead men's bones "Return," says the prophet, "ye transgressors to the heart."—*"Redite, prævaricatores ad cor"* (Isaiah, 46:8). Let us purify our hearts by penance, and adorn them with the graces and virtues of the heart of Mary. O Heart of my Mother! so closely

47

resembling the Heart of Jesus, make our hearts like unto thine!

Second Point.—The heart of Mary is not only the most perfect, but it is also the most tender, compassionate, and merciful heart that ever came from the hands of the Creator. The love which it has for us surpasses as far every known love, as the dignity of the Mother of God surpasses every possible greatness. It is not only a tender, ardent, generous, and heroic love, but it must be acknowledged it is an excess of love which appears to have no bounds. When Jesus Christ desired to show the extent of his Father's love, He says, "God so loved the world as to give his only begotten Son" (John 3:16). "*Sic dilexit.*" It is this that the great Apostle calls the excess of the love of God for man. Now the heart of Mary was capable of the same excess of love; she also delivered up her only begotten Son for the redemption of the world. "*Sic Maria dilexit.*" The united tenderness and solicitude of all mothers for their children can never equal the tenderness and solicitude of the heart of Mary for us. There the just man finds the recompense of his fidelity, the sinner indulgence and mercy, afflicted souls consolation and relief. Oh! truly, what a furnace of charity, what a fire of love is this sacred heart!

Children of Mary, how good and devoted is the heart of your Mother! Behold, it is surmounted by flames, a symbol of the love with which it burns for us; it is pierced with a sword of grief, so that each of us may enter and take refuge; it is encircled with a crown of roses whose perfume embalms our hearts and soothes our woes. How then can we think of this heart without shedding tears of gratitude, and without being filled with love for this good Mother, whose charity is as boundless and fathomless as the ocean.

EXAMPLE

A holy priest in Paris, M. Desgenette, Curé of Our Lady of Victories, saw, with great sorrow, his parish laid waste by irreligion and vice. In a population of twenty-five thousand souls there were but seven hundred communions a year. He was thinking of having recourse to the Sacred Heart of Mary, when one day at Mass, he heard a mysterious voice saying, "Consecrate your Church and parish to the sacred heart of Mary." Obedient to this inspiration, which he believed to come from heaven, he made the act of consecration and promised to pray for all the lost sheep of the house of Israel. His zeal and confidence in the merciful heart of Mary were crowned with the greatest success. Now piety reigns in the midst of his dear children, and crowds fill the once deserted church. Twenty thousand Christians receive the Holy Eucharist, and this number increases each year. Every day wonderful miracles take place which loudly proclaim the power and goodness of the immaculate heart of the Queen of Heaven. The walls of this sanctuary are hung with splendid exvotos, proclaiming some of the numberless graces obtained through her intercession. The name of Our Lady of Victories is known and invoked throughout the world. The Confraternity has extended everywhere, and counts its members by millions: it is a network of immense charity spread over the surface of the globe to save sinners. The small church of Our Lady of Victories stands like a beacon in the midst of Paris, inspire with hope all those who have wounds to be healed, wants to be relieved, or graces to obtain. Glory, love, and gratitude be ever rendered to the precious and merciful heart of Mary.

PRAYER

O most holy heart of Mary, object of the complacency of the adorable Trinity, and worthy of all the veneration of angels and men; maternal heart, which sympathizes with us so keenly in our miseries, listen to our prayers, grant our supplications, and inflame our hearts with that heavenly fire which burns unceasingly in thine own. Never will we forget that thou art the heart of our Mother, and that thou wilt be our assistance in our needs, our consolation in our afflictions, our refuge at the hour of death, and our happiness in eternity. Amen.

NINTH DAY

THE VIRTUES OF MARY

I. Their number.
II. Their perfection.

First Point.—Consider that the possession of one virtue often suffices to render a person attractive: what, then, must be the attractiveness of Mary, who possessed all virtues? Exempt from the stain of original sin, incapable of sinning, not by nature but by the grace of the Holy Spirit, her life was like the sweet odor of incense rising and perfuming all around. For this reason the angel hails her as "*full of grace.*" The Fathers of the Church call her "the center of all virtues." "The other saints," says St. Thomas of Aquinas, "have excelled in some one particular virtue, but the Holy Virgin has excelled in all, so that she has merited to become our model in each." She has had the faith of the patriarchs, the zeal of the apostles, the constancy of the martyrs, the purity of the virgins, the most ardent charity, the most Profound humility, the most courageous patience, the most perfect resignations. "If my eyes contemplate thee, O Mary," exclaims St. Bernard, "thou appearest to me like a delicious garden, perfumed by the sweet flowers of every virtue." A celebrated poet has gone so far as to compare the Blessed Virgin to the heavenly firmament, showing that it would be as difficult to number the stars that stud the canopy of heaven, as the virtues which adorn, with such magnificence, the sacred heart of the Mother of God. "*Tot tibi sunt dotes, virgo, quot sidera coelo*," St. John Chrysostom calls her God's Heaven, and well does she merit this title, since she alone contains more graces, merits, and perfections than the whole celestial court.

Christians, let us remember that the most pleasing homage we can offer to our beloved mother is assuredly the imitation of her virtues. St. John Chrysostom says, "We must forego the title of children of Mary if in our lives no traces of her virtues are found." "I have given you the example. Be you imitators of me as I have been of Jesus my Son." Alas! how little we resemble our Heavenly Mother; how poor are our hearts in virtue! Scarcely have we made the first step in the path of perfection. O admirable Virgin, my true model, I will in future imitate thee, that thy virtues may be reflected in my conduct.

Second Point.—"Since God has willed to choose a Mother," says St. Justin, "it was necessary that he should choose one whose virtues were not ordinary virtues, but heroic, and more perfect than those of all other creatures." "Who," asks St. John Chrysostom, "can show me a being more perfect than Mary, neither the prophets, nor the apostles, nor the virgins, nor any other creature either visible or invisible." Each day, forgetting, like St. Paul, "the things that are behind, and stretching forth to those that are before," she endeavored to render her union with God more intimate, her detachment from creatures more perfect, her humility more profound, her charity more ardent. Each day she advanced in wisdom and age, and grace and merit with God and man, Moreover, had she not the great advantage of having constantly before her eyes Jesus the Model of all sanctity? And who but Mary ever experienced so great a desire to become like to Him? It is therefore with reason that the Church calls her "the Mirror of Justice," which reflects the image of the God-Man, and Bossuet says with truth, "he who sees Mary, sees Jesus."

Alas! we imitate but feebly our beautiful model. We do not go beyond the practice of common virtues instead of aiming at perfection, and weary after placing one foot on the lowest step of Jacob's ladder, we do not seek to ascend higher. This is why we are so weak and wavering, and instead of advancing in the career of perfection, we draw back towards the abyss, and we need seek for no other reason to account for our falls being so frequent and so dangerous. Holy Virgin, make us understand this day that to apply ourselves unceasingly to the attainment of perfection and to make each day new progress in virtue, is a duty enforced by piety and by thy example.

EXAMPLE

A young person wishing to follow in the footsteps of Mary, left her family and the world, entered a religious community, and took the name of Rose. "I wish," said she, "to resemble the Holy Mother of Jesus, whom I have always honored and tenderly loved. I know the Church calls her the Mystical Rose, because her heart, like a sweet smelling rose, exhales the delicious perfume of every virtue which she practiced in the highest degree of perfection. This name will remind me constantly that I ought to imitate so holy a Mother and so finished a model, and become perfect even as the Blessed Virgin is perfect. Each day I will meditate on one of her virtues, and I will make it the rule of my conduct. At the beginning of all my actions I will say, What did Mary do under these circumstances, or what would she have done in my place? *Quid Maria.*"

The young religious imitated her model so faithfully, that she herself became a model to the whole community, which she edified by her tender and increasing piety. Her companions venerated her, and called her St. Rose. She died at the age of fifty-three, rich in sanctity and merit, preserving even after death her freshness and virginal beauty like a newly-opened rose, which impressed all who came to pray beside her holy remains.

Children of Mary, what glory and what happiness will be yours, if you also can resemble in some respects your beloved Mother; what a consolation it will be to you at the hour of death.

PRAYER

O Mary! thy virtues attract and encourage me. I am determined to follow in thy footsteps; but, O Queen of Virtues, O my Mother! my weakness is so great that unless thou dost support me, I shall be incapable of making the least effort to follow thee. Deign, then, O Mary, to stretch forth thy hand to me, and direct my faltering steps: this is the grace I ask of thy maternal goodness. Amen.

TENTH DAY

MARY, MODEL OF FAITH

I. A Lively Faith.
II. An Active Faith.

First Point. —St. Elizabeth, in the salutation she addressed to Mary, speaks only of the greatness of her faith, "Blessed art thou that hast believed, because those things shall be accomplished that were spoken to thee by the Lord" (Luke, 1:45). St. Elizabeth considered that Mary had practiced a heroic faith, because she believed that the Son of God, great and exalted as He is by His divine nature, could so humble and so annihilate Himself, taking, as St. Paul says, the form of a servant, by enclosing Himself miraculously in her virginal womb. St. Liguori, quoting Suarez, says, "that the faith of the Blessed Virgin was firmer than that of all men and angels united. She saw Jesus born in the stable, poor, abandoned, suffering, and nevertheless she believed He was the Creator of the world. She saw Him exiled into Egypt, fleeing from the wrath of Herod, and she believed Him to be the

King of kings, the Almighty God. She saw Him labor as a poor artisan in the carpenter's shop, and still she believed Him to be the master of the universe. She saw Him weep, and yet she believed Him to be the Infinite Beatitude. Lastly, she saw Him die on the ignominious cross between two thieves, and when even the faith of all the disciples faltered, Mary continued to believe Him the immortal God, and that He would rise again." O Mary! how great is thy faith! Nothing can shake it, neither the abasement of the Incarnate Word, nor the perfidy and treason of the apostles, nor the shame of Calvary. Thou hast triumphed over every obstacle, thou hast believed through every trial.

Children of Mary, remember that faith is the foundation of all religion and the groundwork of all virtues. "Without faith it is impossible to please God" (Hebrews, 2:6), and "he that doth not believe is already judged" (John, 3:18). You should then labor unceasingly by prayer to awaken in your soul a spirit of faith, to maintain and enliven it by pious reading, and with the assistance of Mary to render it strong and unshaken. "*Fortes in fide*," O Mary! O Mother of true believers, who wert so happy as to believe, increase our faith; "*Adauge nobis fidem.*"

Second Point.—Not only did the Blessed Virgin

believe with a firm and unwavering faith, she believed also with an active and lively faith. Not only did she listen to the words of the Gospel, meditate and ponder them in her heart, but she put them in practice. Faith was the rule of all her thoughts, her words, her affections, and desires; the motive of all her actions, the source of her strength and constancy in trial and sorrow; it was the mainspring of all her virtues, the support and happiness of her existence. In the various circumstances of her life she was guided by the light of faith, and not by human wisdom and prudence. In all her actions she followed only the inspirations of the grace of God and breathed only for Him. In a word she lived by faith: "*Ex fide vivit.*" Thus she was the most humble, gentle, chaste, charitable of all creatures, and the most accomplished model of all virtues. O great and sublime faith of Mary! who can sufficiently admire and praise you?

Children of Mary, is faith the source and motive power of all your thoughts and works? In all your actions, above all, in the exercise of prayer and the reception of the sacraments, do you endeavor after the example of the Blessed Virgin to be thoroughly penetrated with the spirit of faith? You say you believe, but are your works conformable to your faith? "The devils also believe and tremble," says St. James, and yet they are in hell. How many will be rejected at the last day, not for want of faith, but for neglecting to act according to their belief. O Mary! do not permit me to be of this number. Help me to live according to my faith.

EXAMPLE

A young girl, a victim to worldly pleasures was in a dying state. She was gradually becoming weaker and sinking slowly under the ravages of a wasting consumption. All around her were aware of it; she alone did not realize her hopeless condition. One day she felt that the shadow of death was upon her, and she appeared sad and agitated. Her relatives were grouped around her bed, when suddenly raising in terror her emaciated hands, she let them fall upon her bosom, where she gazed upon them in silence and with fear depicted on her face. At length she exclaimed, weeping bitterly, "See these poor hands of mine; see, they are empty, quite empty. I have believed, I have had the faith, but I have not put it in practice. I have done nothing for God, and I am dying. I am about to appear before my Judge with empty hands, and my faith will serve only to condemn me. Oh! how unhappy I am not to have conformed my life to my belief. Oh! if I could only begin my life afresh and make if more meritorious."

Useless regrets, she was dying with her hands empty—empty of good works. There was despair in her face and tears on her cheeks, and her poor mother wept also. Oh! how true it is that faith without works is a dead faith, which is absolutely of no use for heaven: "*vana est fides vestra.*" Happy then are those souls who have the spirit of faith; unhappy those who are destitute of it. O Mary! cast down upon thy children one spark of thy living and active faith.

PRAYER

O faithful Virgin! speak to my heart the language of faith which has worked so many wonders. May faith be the moving spring of my conversations; may my thoughts, my labors, my pleasures, my meals be regulated by faith. May my whole conduct be deeply imbued with the sweet and strong inspirations of faith. Amen.

ELEVENTH DAY

MARY, MODEL OF HOPE

I. Mary the Mother of Hope.
II. Mary the Mother of the Hopeless.

First Point.—"Hope," says St. Augustine, "springs from faith," and as Mary possessed all the qualities of faith, she had also the gift of a perfect hope. The trials through which it pleased Divine Providence to make her pass, were great and terrible, for her whole life was one long and sorrowful martyrdom, and yet, in the midst of the greatest sufferings, her confidence in God was unshaken. Still more than Abraham, she hoped against all hope. Relying on Divine Goodness, she never consented to the slightest thought of discouragement, either in the stable of Bethlehem, the flight into Egypt, or the anguish of Calvary. She was resigned in all perils, calm in weariness, strong in sorrow, because she had the firm hope that God was her support and consolation. Often she repeated in her heart with the Psalmist, "It is good for me to adhere to my

God, to put my hope in the Lord God" (Ps. 72:28). "Although he should kill me, I will trust in him" (Job, 13:15). Mary, after the Ascension, by the strength of her hope in the promises of Jesus Christ, animated the faith of the disciples, fortified the courage of the martyrs, and supported the infant Church in its struggles and combats. And for this reason, after having called her our Life, our Sweetness, we also call her our Hope, "*spes nostra.*" In the words of Scripture the Church calls her "Mother of Holy Hope;" "*Mater sanctæ Spei.*" A celebrated author has said that "the religion which makes hope a virtue is a divine religion." Yes, indeed, divine, for hope is necessary to all the poor pilgrims of life. "We are saved by hope," says St. Paul. "*Spe salvati sumus*" (Romans, 8:24), and without it our hearts could not live. Hope on, then, O Christians! Hope in a God so good, your loving Father who can and will make you eternally happy. "*Spera in Deo.*" Hope on in Jesus, your Savior, your Brother, who offers you here His merits, and in heaven above an immense weight of glory. Hope on in Mary, your Mother, the best and most powerful of mothers, who leads all her children to eternal happiness. "*Spera in Maria.*"

Second Point.—How much is the sinful soul to be

pitied who after having drunk in iniquity like water, and fallen from one abyss to another, has ended by yielding to discouragement and despair. Oh! wretched despair; it is the executioner of the heart, the hateful crime of Cain and Judas. Where, O sinner, can you find a ray of hope? Be comforted, the heart of Mary is always open to you. Is not Mary the good and tender mother of us all, and as the Holy Fathers call her, "the hope of those who have no hope?" "*Spes desperantium*;" the harbor of the shipwrecked; the refuge of all sinners; the salvation of the agonizing; the shelter of the repentant. Do you not know that hope never dies in the heart of a mother, and the more unhappy is her child, the greater compassion and pity does she feel for it. How many has Mary saved, who appeared irrevocably plunged in crime and despair? How many has Mary restored to hope and repentance who had already cried out with Cain, "My iniquity is greater than that I may deserve pardon" (Gen. 4:13). Banish, then, discouragement and despair, and whatever may be the state of your souls, throw yourselves into Mary's arms. "In her," says St. Ambrose, "there is nothing austere or terrible; she is all sweetness and goodness; she knows not the anger of the Lord," and in Scripture she is never mentioned where there is a question of final impenitence, judgment, and eternal death. Hope then, poor sinner; have confidence, a boundless confidence, an invariable confidence. O Mary, I at least will always hope in thee. I am thy child, O my Mother, and because I hope in thee, I shall never be confounded. "*Ego autem semper sperabo.*"

EXAMPLE

A young man, twenty-six years of age, had lost all his religious principles in Paris. Although dangerously ill he would not allow confession to be spoken of. Time went on, and death rapidly approached. His mother wept and prayed for him. "Since you will not go to confession," said one of his friends to him, "allow me to offer you a picture of the Blessed Virgin. I hope it will bring you happiness." The dying man accepted the picture, he looked at it attentively and remained silent, then turning it round, his eyes rested on the words of St. Ephrem, "*Spes desperantium*, "Mary is the hope of the despairing."

He heaved a deep sigh, and exclaimed, "O yes, merciful Virgin, thou art really the hope of the despairing, and who is in a greater state of despair than I? I am in despair because I am going to appear before the tribunal of Christ, whom I have so grievously offended, for my whole life has been one course of iniquity. O Mary, my only hope and refuge, have pity on my poor soul and save me from despair," and he wept bitterly. A miraculous change had taken place. A priest was brought to the dying man, he made his confession, and despair gave way to the sweetest confidence. At the moment of his death he exclaimed, "Behold the Queen of Heaven—she is come to fetch me; she has obtained for me pardon and mercy." Like a child who throws itself into its mother's arms, he expired in those of Our Lady of Good Hope. O how true it is that none who hope in Mary have ever hoped in vain.

PRAYER

O Immaculate Virgin, Mother of holy Hope, obtain for us this precious virtue which thou didst never relinquish. Then we shall be strong in danger, patient in adversity, valiant in combat, and we shall always be able to say with the Psalmist, "In Thee, O Lord, have I hoped, let me never be confounded" (Ps. 30:1).

TWELFTH DAY

MARY, MODEL OF CHARITY

I. Charity towards God.
II. Charity towards her Neighbor.

First Point.—Faith, Hope, and Charity according to St. Paul, are three great virtues, "but the greatest of these is charity" (1 Cor. 13:13). Now the whole life of the Blessed Virgin was, so to speak, but one act of the love of God. "She loved Him," says St. Bernard, "more than all the seraphim, whose special characteristic is to be inflamed with love." Endowed from the moment of her Immaculate Conception with reason and the knowledge of the Lord, she consecrated herself to Him forever, and loved Him with all her soul. She could with truth say, "*My beloved to me and I to Him*" (Cant. 2:16). "*Thou art the God of my heart and the God that is my portion forever*" (Ps. 72:26). When Mary became the Mother of God, she felt her heart expand, and according to the illustrious Suarez, she loved her Son more than herself, more than all the saints united together. With what ardor and with what devotion she consecrated herself to his service! She shared all his labors, all his sufferings, and humiliations. She followed Him to Calvary; she stood by his cross and watered it with her tears, and without a miracle she would have died of sorrow and of love. After the Ascension of Jesus, the charity of the Blessed Virgin increased yet more. Unceasingly occupied with the thought of her Divine Son, her life became one long ecstasy of love; she lived more among angels than among men. At length consumed with the ardent flames with which her heart was burning she died, according to the opinion of the Doctors of the Church, in an ecstasy of the love of God, and continued in heaven the exercise of love which had been her delight on earth.

Children of Mary, does your love for God resemble Mary's? Is it tender, ardent, and supreme? Does your Savior hold the first place in your heart? Is it entirely his? Oh, how happy would you be if you loved God as St. Augustine did, who cried out, "O Lord, Thou hast made me for thyself alone, and my heart cannot rest until it rests in Thee;" and like St. Francis of Sales, who said often: "If I knew that in my heart there was the smallest fiber which was not steeped in the love of God, I would instantly tear it out." O holy Virgin, *Mother of fair love,* enkindle in our hearts one spark of those ardent flames which consumed thy own, so that we may love our good God, Jesus Christ. *"fac ut ardeat cor meum, in amando Christum Deum."*

*Second Point.—*The tender, generous and motherly love which Mary had for our Lord, rebounds in a manner on the children of men. "She loved them so much," says St. Bonaventure, "that she gave for their salvation more than her life." *"Sic Maria dilexit."* St. Ignatius of Antioch portrays her in these expressive words: "All human miseries," says he, "were hers, and no one could believe her a stranger to them. She felt the sufferings of the infirm and the sick, the privations of the poor, the afflictions of the widow and orphan. Dear though retirement was to her, for her delight was to converse with God, yet when the wants of others called her from her seclusion, she hastened to assist the distressed and console the afflicted. Every suffering awakened her compassion, and her tears were the tears of a mother, who weeps over the woes of her numberless children." We may add that even the enemies of her Son, who were also her enemies, were not excluded from her charity: she openly pardoned them, prayed for them, and adopted them as her children. Raised now to the summit of glory, her heart has expanded still more, and her love for us is greater than that of all the saints put together. With what joy and confidence should not this inspire us? If we wish to prove our right to the title of children of Mary and to merit her love, let us animate ourselves with the same feeling towards our neighbor. Let us love all in Jesus Christ; let us love them as ourselves for the love of God. Let us, above all, love the weak, the little ones, the afflicted, the infirm, the sick, the poor, and those who love us not. It is the great commandment of our Lord, and the mark by which we shall be recognized as the disciples of Jesus and the servants of Mary.

EXAMPLE

During the reign of terror in France, one of its most noble victims ascended the scaffold. His virtuous and courageous wife accompanied him to the place of execution, holding by the hand their little child Louis. The roll of the drums announced the martyrdom of the victim, and whilst his head fell in the dust the heroic woman, taking the poor child in her arms raised him to heaven with trembling hands, and exclaimed, "My God, give to my son the happiness of one day loving the executioner of his father, as Mary at the foot of the cross loved the executioners of her Son. Oh my child, you will forbear to curse him, will you not? You will always bless him who has made you an orphan." The child made the promise. The heroic prayer of this admirable mother was granted; for when twenty-five years of age, the son of the martyr having become a priest, gave bread to his father's executioner, raised his hand to bless and absolve him, and opened for him the gates of heaven. Oh, the power of charity! My God, give us grace to love our enemies as Mary loved hers at the foot of the cross.

PRAYER

O Mary! Mother of pure love, obtain for me the grace of perfect charity, so that we may love God and Jesus thy Son, with all our hearts and souls. Remind us often that we are all brethren; do not permit among thy children discord, hatred, contempt, or indifference, but grant that, united by the bonds of charity, we may have but one heart and one goal. Amen.

THIRTEENTH DAY

MARY, MODEL OF CHASTITY

I. She knew all its value.
II. She avoided all that could endanger it.

First Point.—Purity was always the favorite virtue of Mary. At the age of three she left her home and family, went up to the temple of Jerusalem, and consecrated herself to the Lord by a vow of perpetual chastity. Oh, how beautiful were the first steps of this royal Virgin! To thee, O Holy Mary, was reserved the privilege of planting the first lilies in the garden of the Church and of unfurling the banner of virginity, under which so many virgins, in succeeding ages, have taken their stand. "*Adducentur virgines.*" When the Archangel Gabriel proposed to her to become the Mother of God, she only consented to accept this exalted dignity, after having received the assurance that her divine maternity would not tarnish her virginal purity. Thus she preferred the glory of her virginity to the glory of being the Mother of God. Was it possible to give a greater proof of her love for chastity? St.

Bernard says: "By the most incomprehensible of all mysteries, it was the virginity of Mary that obtained for her the privilege of the divine maternity." "*Virginitate placuit.*" A virgin, by choice and inclination, she found her delight and her happiness in this admirable virtue. A virgin in body and soul, all her thoughts, words, and actions breathed holiness and innocence. A virgin before being a mother, a virgin after having brought into the world her Divine Child, she was always, and will be for eternity, the purest of creatures. The Church calls her the Queen of Virgins, and shows her to us in heaven, walking at the head of that glorious band of virgins who form round the Lamb a guard of honor. "These follow the Lamb whithersoever He goeth, and they sing a new canticle before the throne" (Rev. 14:1, 3, 4).

Whatever our state and condition in life may be, we are all obliged to be chaste and pure. Jesus Christ by his words, Mary by her example, have made it a strict command. St. Ambrose says: "That he who observes chastity is an angel, and he who loses it becomes a demon." Children of Mary, have you always valued and practiced this precious virtue? Alas! perhaps the impure breath of your passions has often tarnished and sullied the beauty of your souls, O, Jesus! create in us a clean heart and renew a right spirit within us. O Mary, mother of chastity, inspire us with a horror of vice and love of virtue.

Second Point—"Mary, more pure than the rays of the sun," says St. Jerome, "had nothing to fear from the poisoned breath of Satan, and yet she lived in continual fear of anything that might tarnish her purity." Although confirmed in grace she distrusted her own strength, as if she was the most fragile of all creatures. She watched over her heart, her thoughts, her words, and all her senses, so as to avoid every occasion of sin. She spoke little, all her words were full of modesty, and her conversation was in heaven. She led an interior life, practiced fasting and mortification, and lived continually in the presence of God, in order to avoid the seductions of the world. According to the beautiful expression of a holy Father, "she breathed only the Lord." "Her whole deportment was angelic," says St. Ambrose, "The purity of her soul was reflected as in a mirror, in her person and countenance. Mary preserved the lily of chastity in all its whiteness, and it is thus that she attained the high degree of glory she now holds in heaven."

If Mary, so pure and so holy, was so careful to preserve this most beautiful and most delicate of virtues, what precautions should we not take who are so weak and inclined to sin? Oh, let us watch over our thoughts, our looks, our words, and fly all dangerous occasions. Let us often ask of God the grace of purity. The wise man says: "And I knew that I could not otherwise be continent, except God gave it" (Wisdom, 8:21). We must, then, have recourse to prayer, for it is a grace that prayer can obtain. Let us also not forget that the saints recommend devotion to Mary as the great means of acquiring and preserving this admirable virtue. This is why the Church places on our lips this beautiful prayer: "Incomparable Virgin, make us chaste and mild; make us lead lives so pure as to bring us to heaven, where we may enjoy the happiness of seeing and loving thy Son." *Mites fac et castos, vitam præsta puram.*

EXAMPLE

A virtuous mother, living in Paris, had great devotion to the Blessed Virgin. She consecrated all her children to her, giving each the name of Mary, so that they might be under the special protection of the Mother of God. This good woman had a great horror of vice, but especially of anything that savored of immodesty. She could not endure the thought that her children should ever be sullied by it, and her generous heart inspired her with the idea of sacrificing herself to preserve them from that misfortune. Many times had she addressed to God the following prayer, conjuring Mary to obtain her request: "My God," said she, "do with me what Thou wilt. Send me the most terrible of torments, but save my children; never permit them to lose their innocence."

A dreadful illness, with which she was seized, gave her reason to hope that her sacrifice was accepted. Her illness lasted five years, during which time she often said to her children: "Be careful to preserve your innocence; it is for that end I suffer and die." At length, satisfied with the heroism of this tender mother, God called her to Himself the 21st day of February, 1834. She gently expired, her hand stretched out to bless her children, her radiant countenance reflecting the angelic innocence of her heart.

Happy mother to have had the courage to make such a sacrifice. Happy children to have had such a virtuous mother. Christians, we too shall be happy if we know how to suffer and endure all, rather than lose the inestimable treasure of chastity.

PRAYER

O Mary, Virgin of virgins, God has chosen thee to be the model of chastity. We hasten then to thee and range ourselves under thy standard. Lead us and protect us so that we may be victorious. Virgin, most pure, virgin most chaste, pray for us and help us. *Virgo purissima, ora pro nobis.* Amen.

FOURTEENTH DAY

MARY, MODEL OF POVERTY

I. How much she valued Poverty.
II. How much she practiced it.

First Point.—Our Lord loved poverty so much that He named it first among the Beatitudes. "Beati pauperes," "Blessed are the poor." Mary esteemed it in no less a degree. "Born of a royal race," says St. Peter Canisius, "she could have lived in ease and comfort on the inheritance of her ancestors; but she contented herself with reserving only a small portion, and the rest she consecrated to the service of the Temple and the relief of the poor." Many authors think that she had made a vow of poverty, as she herself revealed to St. Bridget in these words; "I made from my childhood a vow to possess nothing in this world. All that I could have had I gave to the poor, reserving to myself only what was indispensably necessary for me." Faithful to this spirit of poverty, Mary did not hesitate to take for her spouse St. Joseph, who was poor; and St.

Bonaventure affirms that she supported the Holy Family by the labor of her hands. According to tradition, she did not keep for herself the rich presents that the Wise Men offered to the Child Jesus; she received them to signify her acceptance, and then distributed them to the poor. On the day of the Purification she had no gift to make but the offering of the poor, and yet she shrank not from it. The goods of this world appeared to her mean and despicable. Jesus was her treasure, and He alone her riches. She could say, with the mother of Tobias: "For our poverty was sufficient for us, that we might account it as riches, that we saw our son" (Tob. 5:25).

Happy the Christian soul which, after the example of Mary, despises the vanities, the riches and false goods of this world, in order to be occupied only with heavenly treasures. "*Beati pauperes!*" "Blessed are the poor!" Happy the soul who seeks only Jesus, and desires no other good than Him; she will find even on earth a paradise, according to the beautiful sentiment of St. Francis of Assisi: "My God and my all!" O Mary! thou who wert truly poor in spirit and in heart; thou who didst share the poverty of thy Son, obtain for thy children the grace to love and esteem this treasure. O holy poverty, may we value you as Jesus and

Mary did!

Second Point.—Consider that during, her whole life the Blessed Virgin endured all the rigors of poverty. At Bethlehem the inns were closed against her, she found only a stable and a manger in which to place her Divine Infant, and poor swaddling clothes to wrap around his shivering limbs. What rebuffs and privations had she not to endure in Egypt; perhaps many times when Jesus held out his hand for food she could answer only by her tears. How painful and incessant was her labor at Nazareth to procure sufficient food for each successive day! According to Venerable Bede, after the Ascension of our Lord, Mary, deprived of the only treasure she had possessed in this world, lived only on the alms daily distributed to widows. She could say with Jesus: "The foxes have holes, and the birds of the air nests; but the mother of the Son of Man hath not where to lay her head" (Luke, 9:58). Yes, she whom all nations call Blessed, lived and died poor. She left, according to tradition, no other legacy than two poor garments to the holy women who had assisted her during her life.

Children of Mary, let us love and relieve the poor, for it is written: "Blessed is he that understandeth concerning the needy and the poor:

the Lord will deliver him in the evil day" (Ps. 45:1). "He that giveth to the poor shall not want" (Prov. 28:37); and again, "Charity covereth a multitude of sins" (1 Peter 4:8). Oh, how consoling are these words; would that we could really understand them. Let us give alms during our life, and when the hour of death sounds, Jesus will come and say to us: "I was hungry and you gave me to eat; I was thirsty, and you gave me to drink; I was sick and you visited me" (Matt. 25:35). "Come and take possession of the ineffable joys which your charity has merited in heaven."

EXAMPLE

A celebrated missionary, who was preaching the Month of May, spoke of the love of the Blessed Virgin for poverty and the poor. He ended by saying: "I invite the worst sinner in the congregation to give a good alms to the poor of Almighty God, in honor of Mary the Mother of the poor; and I promise this soul pardon and happiness." At the collection which was made after the sermon, a bank-note was found for a thousand francs. Who had made this rich offering to God and

Mary? No doubt some very guilty soul. Yes, indeed, a most miserable one.

The following day a man came and cast himself at the feet of the preacher, saying, with tears: "Father, yesterday whilst you were preaching on the poverty of Mary, I by chance entered the church, despair was in my soul, I had resolved that very day to put an end to my life, for I no longer valued it. You invited the most unhappy sinner of your audience to give an alms in honor of Mary, I did it, and at that moment I regained hope; I purchased happiness, now I come to obtain pardon; I kneel at your feet, father, hear my confession and help me to bless forever the mercy of God and of Mary." He made his confession and received, together with the pardon of his sins, a proof of the power of charity.

Children of Mary, give alms to the poor in honor of your Divine Mother during this beautiful month, and your hearts will be filled with joy and gladness.

PRAYER

O Mary! obtain for us from Jesus the spirit of poverty and a tender compassion for the sufferings of our neighbor. Grant that God may be our one desire and our only treasure, then, through thy intercession, will be accomplished within us the saving promise of thy Divine Son: "Blessed are the poor in spirit for theirs is the kingdom of heaven" (Matt 5:8).

FIFTEENTH DAY

MARY, MODEL OF PRAYER

I. She prayed without ceasing.
II. She prayed with fervor.

First Point.—Our Divine Master says "that we ought always to pray and not to faint;" and who has performed this great duty more perfectly than Mary? Her whole life was a continual prayer. It began from the first moment of her Immaculate Conception, and her prayer was never interrupted, under any circumstance, till her blessed death. Sleep even, as the Holy Fathers aver, presented no obstacle, for she could say with the spouse in the Canticles, "I sleep and my heart watches." The first years of her childhood were passed in the Temple, where the sweets of prayer took the place of natural affections. She was praying when the Angel Gabriel hailed her as full of grace. She was praying with the apostles in the Cenacle, when the Holy Spirit filled her with the plenitude of celestial treasures. As Mother of God she passed her days in ineffable communication with Jesus, keeping and meditating in her heart all that she heard said of Him. After the Ascension of her Son, she spoke but of heaven, where her loved One reigned. Who can reveal to us the prayer of Mary in the Temple of Jerusalem, beside the manger at Bethlehem, in Egypt, at Nazareth, on Calvary, or when she dwelt with St. John at Ephesus? And now that she is seated at the right hand of her Son in heaven, she never ceases to intercede for the Church, for suffering souls, for poor sinners, and for all her faithful children on earth.

Following the example of Mary, our Mother, let us never weary of prayer. Look at the saints how they hungered and thirsted after prayer; the days were not long enough to spend in this holy exercise, they devoted also to it the silence of the night. Let us pray in the morning, for prayer is then a ray of strength and joy which lightens the toils of the day and draws down the blessings of heaven. Let us pray in the evening, for it is then a canticle of gratitude for blessings received, and an offering of sleep during the night. Let us pray before and after our meals, let us pray in our joys and in our sorrows, in our struggles and in our victories, and then all our actions will be holy and meritorious for eternal life. Sweet virgin teach us to pray without ceasing. "*Doce nos orare*" (Luke, 11:1).

Second Point.—When Mary prayed, it was with so profound a recollection, so tender a confidence, so lively a fervor, that her soul seemed lost in adoration and her countenance, according to ancient tradition, became radiant like that of Moses descending from Mount Sinai. The purest intentions and the most ardent devotion gave to her prayer its great value, and allowed no place for distractions. Neither occupations, nor repose, nor joy, nor sorrows, nor watchings, nor sleep, interrupted her union with God. She was as another angel before the altar, and the angels might well envy the young Virgin, who was more pure and more fervent than all the hosts of heaven. Who could recount the ecstasies, the clear light of her understanding, and the seraphic fervor of her will? Was not her soul like to a golden censer, continually sending up the sweet odors of its fragrance before the throne of God?

Children of Mary, let us here examine our conscience: do we bring to prayer the dispositions which will ensure its success? We pray, indeed, but without attention, fervor, or love. A thousand distractions assail us at the foot of the altar, and the most holy exercises are powerless to fix the levity of our minds. We pronounce the words, we honor God with our lips, but our hearts are far from Him.

Had we but prayed with more faith and recollection, what graces should we not have obtained, what merits should we not have acquired for heaven? O Jesus! O Mary! teach us to pray with fervor, confidence, humility, and perseverance.

EXAMPLE

The following letter, which was written by a soldier, in the west of France, during the Prussian war, affords an excellent proof of the efficacy of prayer: "We were," he writes, "forty soldiers, obliged to leave our sorrowing families, in order to fight the Prussians and save France. But our relatives, our friends, the whole parish, and especially our zealous priest, prayed for us every day. Many were the Masses offered at the altar of the Blessed Virgin for our safe and happy return. Mary prayed also for us, and from heaven above, she, our Mother, blessed us. Before our departure, we received, at her altar, the bread of the strong, the bread of the wayfarer; we appealed to her, saying, 'Mary, thou wilt watch over us; we part from our mothers, but we shall not be left orphans; thou wilt fight for us, conquer with us, and bring us safely back.' Our confidence was not mistaken; so many prayers had not been uttered in vain. Not one of the forty perished, not one was even wounded! We had to endure hunger, cold, the enemies' fire, but all returned safe and sound, whilst many from the neighboring villages had met their deaths."

It was not to be wondered at, owned one who had but little religion, that they returned safe, so many prayed for them, and they had been placed under the protection of the Blessed Virgin. Mary had heard the many supplications, she had watched over her children. Glory, love, and gratitude be given to our heavenly benefactress; we will always love and invoke her.

PRAYER

O Immaculate Virgin! thou whose life was a continual prayer, an unceasing aspiration towards God, obtain for us the spirit of prayer, of which we stand so much in need. We pray; but, alas! our souls, far from being raised to God, cling to earth, and we find ourselves bound by a thousand ties, which we have not courage to break. Obtain for us, O tender Mother, that spirit of faith, of fervor, and of confidence, which raises the soul in prayer. Amen.

SIXTEENTH DAY

MARY, MODEL OF LABOR

I. She labored much.
II. She labored well.

First Point.—The Son of God, to save us, did not shrink from subjecting Himself to the law of labor. He was a carpenter, and the son of a carpenter "*Faber, et fabri filius.*" It was his favorite title. The whole life of Mary was very laborious. Tertullian, who lived shortly after the apostles, distinctly tells us that the Mother of Jesus was one who gained her livelihood by work. In what way did she work? Fenelon, speaking of her says, "How sweet it is to represent to ourselves the august Queen of Heaven, who, according to the custom of the Jewish women, herself made the garments of the Holy Family; those hands which had been accustomed to embroider the beautiful silken hangings of the Temple, were now devoted to sewing the coarse apparel of the carpenter Joseph, or weaving for her Son that seamless robe, for which the soldiers on Calvary cast lots. At other times she might have been seen drawing water for the needs of the household, or preparing the simple meal which she was to share with St. Joseph and her well-loved Son. Her example should dignify labor in the eyes of Christian women." Mary toiled without relaxation; she was, according to the Holy Fathers, never disheartened by the most humiliating circumstances, or the most painful occupations. Jesus, no doubt, could have exempted her from the hard law of labor, but He wished to subject her to it, in order to give us, in her person, a model for our imitation.

All you who labor consider this, and be encouraged. Jesus was an artisan, Joseph a carpenter, Mary labored, working with her hands. Remember well, that in whatever rank of life you may be, it is your duty, honor, and interest, to labor and to avoid idleness, "In the sweat of thy face shalt thou eat bread," said the Lord (Gen. 3:19), "for man is born to labor and the bird to fly" (Job 5:7). Have you hitherto understood this law, and how have you fulfilled it? Have you not often tried to kill time in doing nothing, or been occupied with the merest trifles? Have you not revolted against serious and useful work because it inconvenienced and tired you? Hasten to make up for so much lost time by a laborious and well-occupied life. You will then be able to raise, with confidence, your hands to heaven, and to say with St. Paul: "for such things as were needful for me and them that are with me, these hands have furnished" (Acts 20:34).

Second Point.—Let us represent to ourselves Mary, when employed in work. She made no choice, but accepted all that Providence laid upon her. She did all in the best possible manner, without dilatoriness, which is the mark of idleness; without precipitation, which is the result of impetuosity; without negligence, which is careless as to results; and without indolence, which fears fatigue. Her works, small in appearance, were, in reality, great in the sight of God, because they were exalted by purity of intention and true charity. A holy Doctor of the Church tells us that Mary, in handling her distaff, merited more than even St. Lawrence on the gridiron, owing to the greater spirit of ardent faith which inspired all her actions. She consecrated to God the work of her hands before she commenced it, and asked of Him the grace to perform it well, and during its progress her heart was continually raised to God. "Come, O Lord, to my assistance, bless thy servant, so that all may tend to thy greater glory." After her work she gave thanks to God and devoted herself to prayer. Thus the

Blessed Virgin worked for God and in God; she prayed during labor and labored during prayer; so that she did all things well, and her whole life was a perpetual act of love, an unceasing prayer, according to the words of Holy Scripture, "He that keepeth the law, multiplieth offerings" (Sirach 35:1).

Children of Mary, is it thus you labor? How many long and weary days have you worked which are lost to eternity, because you have acted solely through self-interest, habit, or, perhaps, vain glory? We seek honorable employment, glorious actions, forgetting that sanctity consists in performing well the common and ordinary actions of our state of life. Let us now make the resolution to unite in future all our actions with those of Jesus, offering them to God through Mary's hands, and each one will then merit for us an eternal reward.

EXAMPLE

In a monastery in which St. Romuald was the abbot, there was a young religious, who was very pious and very devout to the Blessed Virgin, through whose intercession he had obtained the grace of a vocation. His was but a short life, for he died three years after he entered the monastery. During his last illness he underwent great mental suffering; he wept often, dreading the judgments of God, and the devil assaulted him with terrible temptations. St. Romuald, who had a high opinion of this religious, was much astonished at his interior trials, and pressed him to tell the cause of these troubles. The novice replied weeping,

"Father, it is true I have labored hard and I hope God will reward me; but, unhappily, I have twice yielded to thoughts of vain glory, instead of offering to God my actions, and doing them all for the love of Him; and now the devil appears to be dragging me down to hell on account of these sins. Oh, Father, pray to God and to the Blessed Virgin for me; obtain my pardon, and tell my brethren in religion to labor only for the greater glory of God."

St. Romuald, without hesitation, assured the religious that his faults had been forgiven. Both invoked, with confidence, the Mother of God, who delivered her client from his fears, and he died the death of the just. What regret should not this example excite in our souls; for, during life, how often does self-love and vain-glory enter into our actions? We sow much, but we have little to reap at the hour of death, because we do not labor from supernatural motives, and in union with Our Savior. O Mary, teach us to labor in a truly Christian spirit.

PRAYER

O God, who, after the fall of our first parents, condemned man to labor for his bread in the sweat of his brow, grant us, after the example of Mary, to labor with perseverance and spirit of faith, so that we may merit the recompense of those who have "borne patiently the burden of the day and the heats" (Matt. 20:12). Amen.

SEVENTEENTH DAY

MARY, OUR MODEL FOR COMMUNION

I. She communicated frequently.
II. She communicated with great devotion.

First Point.—After the Ascension of our Lord, Mary languished with desire to rejoin her Son, her heart yearned for Him, and a miracle alone, says Bossuet enabled her to live separated from Jesus. To console her St. John offered the Holy Sacrifice in her presence, and in ecstasies of love Mary received Jesus in the Eucharist. During the fifteen years that she still remained on earth she never failed to participate in the Sacred Banquet with the rest of the faithful. Each day the Bread of Angels became the food of the Queen of Angels. Each day the Bread of Life formed the nourishment of her who had given life to her God. Thus was she compensated for the absence of her beloved Son, Jesus. Thus were renewed for her the joys of her maternity, and, like the apostles, Mary persevered in the breaking of bread.

Children of Mary, frequent Communion should

be your happiness. The Blessed Virgin redoubles her love for you when she sees her Divine Son reposing in your hearts. To communicate frequently is to comply with the express wish of Jesus Christ, "whose delights are to be with the children of men" (Prov. 8:30), and who threatens, with eternal death, those who do not approach the Heavenly Banquet. Lastly, frequent Communion is a necessity for our souls, which cannot practice virtue, overcome the world or the devil, without constantly receiving the bread of the strong. "Let us live," says St. Augustine, "in such a manner as to be worthy to communicate daily." O Mary, make us hunger and thirst after this Bread of Life, "the corn of the elect, and wine springing forth virgins" (Zach. 9:17.)

Second Point.—Who can tell the sentiments with which the heart of Mary was penetrated when this mystery of love was accomplished within her. Communion was for her a renewal of the Incarnation; the Heavenly Virgin prepared herself to receive the Divine Eucharist, as she had prepared herself for that first mystery of our salvation, that is, with the ardor of holy desires, and, above all, with a profound humility and a spotless purity." *"Virginitate placuit, humilitate concepit,"*— "By her

Virginity she pleased Him, by her humility she conceived Him." Could we have penetrated into that sanctuary, adorned by the hand of the Holy Virgin, and have assisted at the Holy Sacrifice offered by the beloved disciple, we should have seen Mary absorbed in the most profound sentiments of adoration, fervor, and love, calling on Jesus with all the fervent desires of her heart. We should have seen St. John reverently placing his beloved Savior on her Virginal lips. "O Mother! behold thy Son," "*Ecce filius tuus,*" and Mary, absorbed in the sense of her lowliness, repeats the canticle of humility, "*Magnificat.*" She glorifies the Lord, and adores Him with all the powers of her heart and soul. Oh! what a spectacle for even the angels to contemplate.

Children of Mary, if you wish to learn how to communicate well, reflect on the Communion of Mary, your Mother, and strive to imitate her profound respect and adoration, her acts of the most sublime virtues, her humble faith, and ardent chanty. To supply all that is wanting to your souls when you approach this Divine Banquet, offer to the Eucharistic God the tenderness and ardor of the Immaculate Heart of His Mother. This is a favorite practice of those who are true servants of Mary.

EXAMPLE

A young girl, twelve years of age, had great devotion to Jesus in the Blessed Sacrament. Her desire and happiness were to receive Him at the Holy Table, and in order to perform this great action well, she imagined to herself the Blessed Virgin and St. Joseph at her side, adoring Jesus in her heart. She wished to communicate every day, but her confessor did not permit it, on account of her tender age, so she was obliged to content herself with devoutly hearing Mass and making a Spiritual Communion, which she did, shedding many tears, so great was her desire to be united to her God. The Lord deigned to work a miracle to satisfy the wishes of this angelic child. One day, when she abandoned herself to her pious grief, and was watching with tearful eyes the persons who approached the Holy Table, a Host descended visibly from on high and remained suspended over her head, to the great astonishment of all who beheld it. The priest, greatly surprised, paused, then holding out the paten he received the Sacred Host on it, and with deep emotion, communicated the pious child, whose happiness was so great that, transported with divine love, she expired in the heavenly embrace of Jesus in the Blessed Sacrament.

Oh! did we but hunger and thirst after our Lord as the saints did, He would give Himself to us more frequently, and we should be fully satisfied and consoled. O Holy Virgin, excite in our hearts an ardent desire of frequent Communion.

PRAYER

O Mary! ark of the New Covenant, first Tabernacle of the Word made Flesh, thou who didst so often and with so much love receive Jesus in the Blessed Sacrament, obtain for us the necessary dispositions to make always holy and fervent Communions. We are not worthy of assisting at the Banquet of the Angels, but say only one word to thy Divine Son, and we shall approach with confidence. Amen.

EIGHTEENTH DAY

MARY, MODEL OF DEVOTION TO THE PASSION

I. She meditated on the mystery of the Passion.
II. She visited the scenes of the Passion.

First Point.—It is related of some of the saints that they bore the symbols of the Passion engraved on their hearts; of other saints it was said that divine love had inscribed the sacred name of Jesus on their breasts in letters of gold. We can say of Mary, that her heart was like a Calvary, where the sacrifice of the cross was unceasingly renewed in spirit. According to some of the Fathers of the Church, her principal occupation during the last years of her life was to repass in her memory the cruel history of the Passion of her only Son. She thought of it continually, and this thought penetrated her with love and gratitude for the spotless victim, with horror for sin, and with tenderness for man. This was revealed by the Blessed Virgin to St. Bridget, who thus relates it: "During the time that I lived after the Ascension of my Son, I never ceased to think of His sufferings and death. His Passion was so engraved in my heart, that whether I reposed, or whether I labored, its remembrance was always present to my memory, and every place was to me a Calvary."

As all the saints were remarkable for being devout to the Passion of Our Lord, we should also make it the object of our especial devotion. St. Bonaventure exclaims, "Oh, how good it is to be with Jesus crucified. I will make here three tabernacles—one in His hands, one in His feet, and the third in His wounded side. There will I rest, there will I live, and there will I die." "If," adds the same saint, "you desire to draw down upon yourselves grace upon grace, and to advance in virtue, devote yourselves each day to this holy exercise."

Children of Mary, study this truth, and remember that a single tear shed by a loving heart at the feet of the crucified God is a thousand times sweeter than all the pleasures of the world. Then you will desire with the great apostle to have no other glory or joy than that of the cross of our Lord Jesus Christ. O Jesus crucified, bestow on us, like St. Paul, a heart that can say, "the charity of Christ presseth us."

Second Point.—The Blessed Virgin was not content with meditating in her heart on the sorrowful mysteries of the Passion. Each day, according to tradition, she visited those places sanctified by the presence and sufferings of Jesus: the garden of Olives where He sweat blood; the Pretorium where He was scourged and condemned to death; the road to Calvary, where He fell three times under the weight of our sins; Golgotha where He breathed His last sigh on an infamous gibbet, and the sepulcher where His holy body was laid when taken down from the cross. Venerable Bede says she watered with her tears these sacred places, and kissed them with her virginal lips. It is related that some pious pilgrims expired when they kissed the sacred footprints of the Savior. Was it not then miraculous that the Holy Virgin should kiss a thousand times these same footprints and yet not die? It appears that Mary would never go far from the places sanctified by the Passion of her Son, and she chose her tomb near these dear and venerated spots. Thus the Blessed Virgin, separated from her Son, found her only consolation in treading that *Via Dolorosa.* It was no doubt her example that incited the holy women of Jerusalem and the early Christians to visit and contemplate that sorrowful way marked by the footsteps of the Savior.

In memory of these devout pilgrimages of Our Lady of Dolors, the Church has instituted the holy practice of the Way of the Cross. This pious exercise, enriched with numerous indulgences, should be particularly dear to the children of Mary, since she was the first to teach it to us. Let us profit by a devotion so consoling and advantageous for ourselves, and for all the faithful living and dead. Oh! precious way of the cross, you shall always be my delight, and shall become to me the road to heaven. O Mary, I will unite myself to thee in performing this devotion; teach me to do it with love, piety, and compunction.

EXAMPLE

A mission was being given in a small parish, and the faithful came in crowds to hear the word of God, and obtain pardon of their sins. Three men alone refused to profit by this great grace. They had promised each other and sworn that they would not enter the church, and more especially that they would not go to confession.

The wife of one of the men came one day to the mission priest and told him what grief the conduct of her husband caused her.

"Have you any children?" asked the missioner.

"I have two," she replied, "who are still quite young."

"Very well, bring them to the church, and with them make devoutly the Stations of the Cross, ask for the conversion of your husband through the sufferings of Jesus and Mary, and I promise you that you will obtain it."

Each day at noon when the church was the least frequented, the virtuous wife came with her two children and knelt before the Tabernacle, afterwards making the Stations of the Cross. At each station the poor mother wept, and the little children exclaimed with their hands extended towards the image of the Savior, "O Jesus, convert our father." What could be more touching than such a sight, worthy at once of the admiration of heaven and earth. The angels doubtless received the prayers and tears of the mother and children and carried them to the throne of mercy, for the day before the close of the mission the hardened sinner knelt at the feet of the priest, and together with his wife joyously received the Holy Eucharist. Afterwards calling his children to him, he affectionately embraced and blest them. Oh, holy way of the Cross, a way salutary to all, but especially to sinners.

PRAYER

O Mother of Sorrows, who didst so often meditate on the Mystery of the Passion of thy Divine Son, thou who wast the first to tread those spots hallowed by His sufferings, teach us to meditate and practice like thee this holy and salutary devotion. Grant that in it we may find the grace of conversion for sinners, perseverance for the just, and relief for the souls in purgatory. Amen.

NINETEENTH DAY

MARY, OUR MODEL IN SUFFERING

I. How much she suffered.
II. In what way she suffered.

First Point—Who can describe the sufferings of Mary? Alas, they were continual and excessive. *Continual*, the martyrs in general had to suffer but for a few hours or for a few days, rarely did their sufferings extend over months, but the whole life of the Blessed Virgin was one protracted agony, a long and perpetual martyrdom. The sword of sorrow predicted by Simeon was piercing her heart continually, and the bleeding tragedy of Calvary, described in Scripture, was unceasingly before her eyes and present to her mind. She could literally appropriate to herself the words which David places in the mouth of the Divine Redeemer, "My life is wasted with grief and my years in sighs: my sorrow is continually before me" (Ps. 30:11; Ps. 37:18).

Her sufferings were excessive. St. Bernard assures us that Mary suffered in her soul more than all the martyrs put together. He even goes so far as to say that had the sufferings which Mary alone endured been divided amongst all others, they were sufficient to have caused their deaths. It is then with reason that the Church calls Mary the Queen of Martyrs: *Regina Martyrum.* O Daughter of Jerusalem, O Mother of Sorrows, to what shall we compare thee? Where shall we ever find a sorrow like to thy sorrow? We must say with the prophet in the Lamentations, "For great as the sea is thy sorrow" (Lam. 2:13). *Magna est velut mare.*

Children of Mary, let us ever feel a tender compassion for the Queen of Martyrs, and let us never forget the sorrows of our Mother. Let us sometimes reflect that it is we who have been the cause of her long and cruel martyrdom, and when we have crosses to bear, let us unite them to hers and tread courageously in the footsteps of the Son and the Mother. Let us remember that it "is through many tribulations we must enter into the kingdom of God" (Acts. 14:21). "Oh! how sweet it is to suffer" exclaims St. Bernard, "when by our sufferings we merit eternal happiness, and avoid torments that never end."

> *"Eja Mater fons amoris*
> *Me sentire vim doloris*
> *Fac ut tecum lugeam."*

Second Point.—If of all the martyrs the Blessed Virgin was the most tried, she was also the most courageous and resigned. Never was she known to murmur or yield to discouragement; not when Simeon predicted that a sharp sword should pierce her heart; not when she was forced to fly with her Child to Egypt, and dwell there during seven years; not when she had the trial of losing Him for three days in Jerusalem; and, lastly, not even when she was present at the great Sacrifice of Calvary. Neither the abyss of her sorrows, nor the sight of death, neither the fury of men nor the rage of demons could discourage her, esteeming herself happy to drink with Jesus of the chalice of His humiliation, and to drain it even to the dregs. On that fearful day she stood at the foot of the cross like a priest before the Altar of Sacrifice. "*Stabat Mater.*" Knowing that it was the will of God that Jesus should die to save the world, she cooperated with Him with all the powers of her soul. "Heavenly Father," she exclaimed, "take Thy sword and strike the victim. In taking from me my Son, Thou dost pierce my heart, but I accept all for thy glory and the salvation of the world." Oh! what a wonderful example of patience and resignation does not Mary give us. O generous heart of Mary, how great thou art!

Alas! how little do we resemble this perfect model. A single interior trial, a single affliction, the slightest suffering is sufficient to dishearten us, and to cause us to murmur and complain. Thus it is that we lose all the fruits of our trials and sufferings. Why are we so weak? Ah! it is because we do not know how to lean on the cross as Mary did. "*Stabat juxta crucem.*" If we thought often of the sufferings of the crucified God, it would support us in our trials, and instead of pitying ourselves, we should say with the Blessed Virgin, "Father, thy will be done on earth as it is in heaven."

EXAMPLE

In the year 1842, in a little town in France, there lived a pious woman who grieved for the loss of her only son, who, after a short and painful illness, had died. She ate and slept but little, her health began to give way. This poor mother was present at a sermon preached on the Feast of the Compassion of the Blessed Virgin. The preacher had taken for his text, the words of Jeremias, "Oh, all ye that pass by the way, attend and see if there be any sorrow like to my sorrow" (Jer. 1:12).

After speaking of the sufferings of the Blessed Virgin, the preacher addressed himself in touching words to those amongst his hearers who were mothers. "Who is there amongst you, O ye Christian mothers, listening to me, who dares to compare her grief to that of Mary? Mary, in her sorrow, was firm and courageous; Mary stood at the foot of the cross, '*Stabat.*' Oh, all you who suffer and weep, take your stand with Mary at the foot of the cross; be brave in the midst of your grief."

These words, which the disconsolate mother applied to herself, comforted her afflicted heart; she fell on her knees before the cross which surmounted the Tabernacle, recited the Stabat Mater, and uniting her sufferings with those of the Mother of Sorrows, rose up full of courage. From that time forward, she became a model of resignation. All you who are in affliction look at Jesus on the cross, and at Mary at the foot of that cross. What an excess of sufferings and what an excess of resignation will you behold. Lean on the cross, recite devoutly the Stabat, and you also will find comfort.

PRAYER

O Lord Jesus, now that we know the advantages of sufferings, we will no longer complain of them, but, rather, we will say to Thee, with St. Augustine, "Here cut, here burn, spare me not in time so that Thou spare me in eternity. O Mary, Mother of Sorrows, Queen of Martyrs, obtain for us patience and resignation. Amen.

TWENTIETH DAY

MARY IS THE REFUGE OF SINNERS

I. She is their Mother.
II. She is their advocate.

First Point.—Mary is a Mother; she loves us as she loved Jesus; but those among her children, those who are the most unhappy, the most guilty, the most ungrateful, those are they whom she loves with the most tender and compassionate love. According to St. Bernard and St. Bonaventure, just souls call to the remembrance of Mary, the Child Jesus as she saw Him at Nazareth, gentle, humble, affectionate, in a word, full of grace; and touched by this likeness, she showers down on them a thousand favors. But sinners recall to her memory Jesus on Calvary, Jesus scourged, crowned with thorns, bruised and cold, as when she received Him in her arms. Did she not love Him then? Oh, yes, she loved Him then even more. Thus also does she love poor sinners, her guilty children, especially those who have not entirely forgotten her; there is still hope for them; she will save them. Take courage, then, poor sinners, however deeply you may be sunk in crime; beware of abandoning yourselves to despair. No, indeed, all is not lost, your case is not hopeless, you still have a Mother, whose mercy surpasses your iniquities more than the heavens are exalted above the earth. Were you even a thousand times more guilty, still take courage. One tear shed by Mary, one drop of the blood of her Son can make your soul whiter than snow. Say but a word of prayer, heave but a sigh, and the Blessed Virgin will come to your aid. Have confidence then, an unlimited confidence. *O peccator ne diffidas.*

Children of Mary, let us also show compassion to poor sinners, they are our brethren, our unhappy brethren. They have lost the life of grace, the arm of an angry God is raised above their heads, they are walking on the brink of a bottomless pit, in danger at any moment of falling headlong into it. Let us pity their lamentable state, let us stretch out to them a helping hand, and if they are poor or sick, let us hasten to their aid. But ought we not to compassionate still more their spiritual miseries? The charity that we show towards sinners is most pleasing to God and most meritorious, for the Holy Spirit declares, "He who causeth a sinner to be converted from the error of his way, shall save his soul from death, and shall cover a multitude of sins" (James 5:20).

Second Point.—Another motive, well calculated to increase the sinner's confidence in Mary is, that she is not only their mother, but their mediatrix with God. As a mother seeks to reconcile two children who are at variance, so does the august Virgin endeavor to reconcile the sinner, her child by adoption, to Jesus her Son by nature, She prays to Jesus for the poor sinner, for his sake she recalls the remembrance of those blessed days, when the God-Man lay in her aims, as if to make her the dispenser of his graces, and she supplicates Him to forget the sinner's rebellion and ingratitude. At the same time, by many secret inspirations of grace, she fills the heart of her disobedient child with sentiments of confidence and compunction. Truly it seems a combat between God, who is about to strike, and our advocate, who stays His arm; between the Son who would destroy, and the Mother who would save, and the Mother is ever victorious. "Oh, infinite goodness of our God!" exclaims St. Bonaventure, "who has provided so powerful an advocate for such wretched criminals, in order that by her help all may be saved."

Children of Mary, in how many ways can we

not exercise charity towards poor sinners? We can pray for them, offer for their conversion our communions, our good works, our daily pains and trials; we can give them good advice, and edify them by good example. If we sincerely loved our neighbor, we should know how to succor him in his spiritual infirmities. God Himself would help us, and, with the assistance of his grace, we should be able to save those erring souls whom He has purchased at the cost of his Blood.

EXAMPLE

A missioner writing to a friend, thus relates an incident which had happened to him:—"I wished," said he, "to avail myself of the occasion of my ordination to the priesthood, to bring back my father to his religious duties, and induce him to frequent again the sacraments, for since the time of his first Communion he had done nothing. I spoke to him on the subject, but was answered coldly, "I cannot do it, for I have been too great a sinner."

This reply dismayed me, and I scarcely dared hope for his conversion, which, up to this time, I had so ardently desired. Two of my fellow-students, to whom I made known the distress of mind I was in, said to me: "If your father is so great a sinner, we must recommend him to the Blessed Virgin, who is the sure refuge of sinners. Let us begin a novena; we will join our prayers to yours, and have confidence." I followed this good advice, I prayed earnestly to her, who is never invoked in vain, to have pity on the soul of my poor father.

During the novena, I ventured to speak again to him on this delicate matter, a great and unexpected change had taken place, my father no longer made any opposition, but said: "I will make my confession, I will return to God." I conducted him to a priest with whom I was acquainted, who instructed him, heard his confession, and on the happy day of my first Mass I had the consolation of seeing my father approach and receive Communion from my hands. He was deeply moved, and God alone knows the joy with which my soul was inundated on that never-to-be-forgotten day. Glory be to Mary, the refuge of poor sinners, eternal gratitude and love to this tender Mother, whose devoted child I am resolved to be all the days of my life.

PRAYER

Multiply, O Mary, multiply without ceasing the acts of thy great goodness towards so many blind and reckless souls, who are hurrying to their eternal doom. Work a miracle in their favor, change their rebellious souls into docile and submissive children, so that they may forever praise and bless thee with Jesus, thy Divine Son, for all eternity. *Refugium peccatorum, ora pro nobis.*—Refuge of sinners, pray for us Amen.

TWENTY-FIRST DAY

MARY, COMFORTER OF THE AFFLICTED

I. She compassionates our sorrows.
II. She softens their bitterness.

First Point.—Those who comfort others should themselves have passed through trials. "I have known sorrow," said one who had suffered, "therefore I have compassion upon the distressed." What consolations have we not then a right to expect from Mary, who has been the most afflicted of all women, and whom the Church calls the comforter of the afflicted. With the one exception of sin, there is not any sorrow which she has not experienced? Like Jesus, she has borne the weight of the punishment of sin, she has felt all its bitterness on Calvary. Full well she knows the anguish which can rend the heart, the anxiety which can torture the mind, the sufferings which can crush the body. "No, indeed," exclaims St.

Antoninus, "there is not amongst the saints in heaven one whose heart is capable of compassionating our sufferings like the heart of the ever Blessed Virgin.

Children of Mary, you too have troubles and afflictions, but why do you confide them to creatures, instead of entrusting them to the compassionate heart of your Mother? "Men," says Job, "are all troublesome comforters" (Job, 16:2), *consolatores onerosi*, who know not how to feel our woes nor alleviate them. If you speak to them of your sufferings, they will not understand you, and you will lose all the merit of them; if you tell your anguish to your own heart, nature will complain, and will blame both God and man. Go then, ye afflicted, all you who suffer, go to Our Lady of Sorrows, tell her all your distress, weep, if you will, she will console you. "Be comforted, my child," will she say to you, "I have passed through the same trials; my soul, which a sword has pierced, understands full well thy grief. This chalice, which is to thee so bitter, I have drank it to the dregs; this cross, which seems to thee so heavy, I have carried it with my Son to Calvary. Be comforted, I am at thy side; I number thy sighs, I gather thy tears, and heaven will be thy recompense. "O Mary! O compassionate Mother, be always our support in this valley of tears. *Consolatrix afflictorum, ora pro nobis,*—Comforter of the afflicted, pray for us.

Second Point.—"Come to me, all you that labor and are burdened, and I will refresh you," says the Lord (Matt 13:38). This tender, loving Mother speaks to us the same language, and, moreover, it would seem as if Jesus Himself would not give comfort to the afflicted except through Mary. There is no ill that this unfailing treasury of consolation cannot soothe or cure; no distress that she does not share; no tears that she cannot wipe away; nor is there a soul bowed down with grief into the depths of which she cannot penetrate, to shed a ray of hope. St. John Damascene compares her to a public hospital, which he says "God has opened for all the sufferings and miseries that overwhelm mankind, and where, if there are not always cures, at least some alleviation for, suffering found." Who is there amongst us, who, in the time of trial, has not experienced a hundred times the mysterious effects of the protection of Mary? In how many ways has she not extended to us her hand and supported us in our weakness? The prayer we addressed to her was hardly ended, when we already felt that she was near at hand, and in proportion as our sufferings were great, so much greater was her care for us. Oh, what love and tenderness is there not in the heart of our beloved Mother!

True charity softens the heart towards those who suffer, for suffering has a claim upon our compassion. It is related that a Pagan once said, "I am a man, and nothing that regards man is indifferent to me." With still greater reason should a child of Mary be actuated by charity towards others, and entertain for all, without distinction, feelings of benevolence and pity. Let us then make the resolution to sympathize with, to visit and console, to the best of our ability, all who are in affliction. A word spoken in kindness, a word of pity, a small alms, a short prayer, is often sufficient to raise and cheer a prostrate and disheartened soul. Virgin most clement, comforter of the afflicted, give us a tender and compassionate heart.

EXAMPLE

A lady, a votary of the world, had the grief of losing her child, and nothing could console her or alleviate her sorrow, which bordered on despair. She could neither sleep nor eat, and her family were deeply concerned at her distress. A young man, an artist by profession, and one who was deeply imbued with religious feelings, had the happy thought of painting a portrait of the child whose loss she deplored, with the hope that the sight of the loved features might cause a salutary reaction, but he also feared that the sight of the picture might increase her anguish and despair. Acting from a pious inspiration, he painted two pictures of equal dimensions. One represented the much-regretted child; the other Mary the Mother of Sorrows, holding in her arms her Son, Jesus, pale, bleeding, and dead. At the bottom of this picture the artist had written the words, "Her loss was greater than yours."

The poor mother at the sight of her child's portrait fainted, but again becoming conscious, the image of the Mother of Sorrows met her eyes. "Yes, she has lost more than I, and yet she does not weep; she stands at the foot of the cross: *Stabat*." From that moment her tears ceased to flow, never again was she heard to murmur, and she reverently kept the two pictures, unwilling that they should ever be separated. Children of Mary, when death snatches from you one whom you love, or when Divine Providence sends a heavy cross to bear, look at Mary on Calvary and say, "She has lost and suffered more than I have, and yet she is resigned:

"*Stabat.*" This thought will ever be a comfort and support to you.

PRAYER

O Mary, powerful comforter, with entire confidence, in the midst of our sorrows, we throw ourselves at thy feet. Thou wilt listen to our sighs, favorably receive our prayers and dry our tears, because thou hast known the weight of suffering. Thou wilt console us, because thou art all good and all powerful, and because thou dost love so tenderly thy poor children here below. Amen.

TWENTY-SECOND DAY

MARY, HEALTH OF THE SICK

I. She cures corporal infirmities.
II. She cures spiritual infirmities.

First Point—Consider, children, of Mary, that diseases and infirmities of all kinds are the sad lot of poor human nature. From the cradle to the tomb tears and sufferings are our inheritance. Nevertheless, let us take courage; there is a saving name that shines brightly for all, for the sick man on his bed of pain, for the poor patient given over by physicians, for all who are unhappily bowed down under the weight of suffering. This name is no other than the name of Mary, whom the Church calls Our Lady of Good Help, Our Lady of Deliverance, the health and salvation of the sick. She can say with greater truth than the apostle Paul, "Who is weak and I am not weak? who is scandalized and I am not on fire?" (2 Cor. 11:29.) From the heart of the Mother, as before from the person of her Son, goes forth a saving virtue which cures all ills. Yes, by the intercession of our Queen, the lame walk, the blind see, the deaf hear, the paralyzed recover the use of their limbs, the dying return to life. The walls of her sanctuaries are covered with votive offerings, silent witnesses to the gratitude of those she has miraculously cured. How many mothers have implored and obtained from her the life of an only son, or a much-loved daughter? How often have we heard persons say, that after praying to Mary she cured them of a painful disease, that she cured a parent, a friend, or a benefactor, whose life had been despaired of. Thus have the most acute sufferings and maladies of every kind been alleviated by her, who has not in vain been called Our Lady of Good Help, for she draws as she wills, from the heart of the Divine Physician, the balm which heals and cures our souls.

Children of Mary, behold here a fresh motive of confidence. Have recourse, then, to Mary in all your infirmities; do yet more, follow her example, visit and comfort the sick, teach them how to sanctify their sufferings, how to resign themselves to the will of God, how to make frequent acts of patience, of contrition, and desire of heaven. You may rely on the gratitude of Jesus, who holds as done to Himself what you do for the least of his disciples, and who will say to you on the Day of

Judgment, "Come ye blessed of my Father, I was sick and you visited me," (Matt. 25:36). *Infirmus fui et visitastis me.* "Possess you the kingdom prepared for you from the foundation of the world." (Matt. 25:34).

Second Point.—Besides these corporal infirmities, Mary feels a yet greater compassion for the diseases of the soul. How many sick Christians are there, whose souls are weak in faith, in piety, and fervor, who in the spiritual order lead only a languishing life; who exhibit every appearance of lukewarmness, and who will soon, perhaps, fall into the abyss of mortal sin. It is chiefly for such souls that Mary delights to intercede with her Son. She loves to listen to their sighs and to grant their prayers. If aching bodies, paralyzed limbs, and injured sight, have been cured through her intercession, how many tepid hearts have also regained their former fervor; how many spiritually blind have again found the light of faith; how many paralyzed souls have obtained strength to walk with fresh vigor in the path of God's commandments. In fine, how many weak souls have been spiritually cured and changed into courageous and fervent Christians. But, alas, too often these lukewarm Christians are not aware of the state they are in, they do not desire their cure, and they do not think of asking for it, through the powerful intercession of Mary.

Children of the best of mothers, let us enter into our own hearts, let us examine seriously if we too are not in this sad state, and if there are not in us signs of the same tepidity. How sad a state it is for a soul to be indifferent towards a God who merits so much love; to feel no eagerness for his glory or zeal for his interests, and to have for Mary but a barren affection, without endeavoring to imitate her virtues. How easy is it to pass from the sleep of tepidity to the slumber of death. O good Mother, vessel of singular devotion, dissipate the illusions of our understandings, melt the ice of our frozen hearts and renew our souls in the fervor of thy service. We will live henceforth in that spirit of sacrifice and generosity, which is the proof of true love, and the distinctive mark of thy devoted servants.

EXAMPLE

A criminal, condemned to death, asked a few minutes before mounting the scaffold, to see a religious of a certain Order, whom he named. The religious came at once, and the condemned man addressed him thus: "Father, I belonged to your Order, I have worn the habit you wear and made my profession. I was for some time a good religious, and I can assure you that so long as I faithfully observed the rule, so long as I had great devotion to the Blessed Virgin, I was happy, nothing was irksome to me, I performed the most difficult tasks with ease and with joy. Oh, what an enviable lot was mine! But, unhappily, I began little by little to grow lax, I fell into a state of tepidity, I rarely thought of invoking Mary, and from that time I became disgusted with the exercises of the community. Unfaithful to my obligations, the yoke of my holy faith became insupportable to me, and I secretly left the monastery and threw aside my religious habit. Alas! my fate became more deplorable, for I fell into the worst of crimes, and now you see to what my sins have led me: doubtless, I should have died impenitent, if the Blessed Virgin had not taken pity on my poor soul, blessed be her name forever. I sent for you, Father, so that you might tell the religious of your Order what I have made known to you; convince them that tepidity leads to the greatest excesses, and may my example be of use to them."

Learn, O children of Mary, that a solid and

constant devotion towards your tender Mother is an unfailing means of acquiring fervor and perseverance in the service of God.

PRAYER

Merciful Virgin, cast thy compassionate eyes on the sick and weak; strengthen their courage, obtain for them relief and health, but above all, cure tepid and languishing souls, in order that they may love and serve thy Divine Son with new fervor and greater generosity. Amen

TWENTY-THIRD DAY

MARY, PATRONESS OF A GOOD DEATH

I. For the just.
II. For sinners.

First Point.—How terrible is the moment of death, on which depends eternity; but the Queen of Heaven will come then to the assistance of her faithful servants, and to all who have in life merited her protection by their filial love and devotion, she will soften the terrors of that day, and assist them in their passage to eternity. St. Liguori says that on that day, when she had both the consolation and the grief of assisting at the last moments of her Son, she received the office of ministering to the souls of the predestined at the hour of death. All you who have so often called on Mary to help you at your last hour, can you fear that she will ever forget either your title to her protection or her duty towards you? On the contrary, believe that she will stand at the foot of your dying bed as she once stood at the foot of the cross to soften your agony and to receive your last sigh. The Blessed Virgin, having appeared to St. Gertrude, said to her: "During life I undertake to give to my servants all necessary graces, but at death I come to them in person, and by a single look I put to flight the powers of hell; never will I abandon, at this dread hour, those who have honored me." It is a well known fact that all who in life were animated with a filial confidence in Mary leave this earth without regret, and give, at the hour of death, the most consoling signs of salvation. A great saint said, "Never has there been seen, and never will there be seen a true servant of the Blessed Virgin making a bad end." It is also to be remarked that a number of saints renowned for their devotion to Mary have had the privilege of dying on some of the feasts of the blessed Virgin.

Remember, Christians, that in order to die as true Children of Mary, it is necessary to live as such, for, ordinarily speaking, death is but the echo of life. "In what place soever the tree shall fall, there shall it be" (Eccles. 11:3). Let, then, your practice be detachment from the world, vigilance over your hearts, the practice of good works, the imitation of the virtues of your heavenly Mother. Let us merit by the observance of a truly Christian life a death precious in the sight of God; let us so live that after death it may be said of each of us, he was a true disciple of Jesus and a faithful servant of Mary. O merciful Virgin, obtain for us the grace to live in thy service, and die a holy death in thy maternal arms.

Second Point.—Though Mary bestows her favors in preference on the just, she will not on that account abandon the dying sinner. How often has she sought him in his wanderings; how often has she not stayed the arm of her Son ready to strike. Would she then abandon him when on the verge of falling into the bottomless pit for all eternity? Oh, no! Her maternal heart, moved with pity at the sight of the fearful danger which threatens, will plead his cause with Him who came to save, not the just, but sinners, and she will obtain for the poor sinning soul sentiments of confidence and repentance. A mother would pass through fire and water to save her child, and Mary is truly the Mother and the sure refuge of sinners. How many unrepenting souls have at the approach of death owed their salvation to this merciful Virgin? When the ministrations of a priest had been refused, when the image of Christ crucified was rejected, when neither wife nor children could obtain anything from the hardened heart of the sinner, and his shortening breath would only utter the words that as he had lived so did he wish to die, it was then that all present had recourse to Mary, the Mother of Mercy, the hope of those who have no hope, the help of the abandoned, and behold the heart of the dying man is changed and softened. The priest he had repulsed is recalled, and recommending himself to the prayers of those around, he makes a sincere confession of his sins, and dies calmly like the just man, pronouncing the sweet name of Our Lady, Patroness of a good death.

Children of Mary, pray often for the agonizing. Eighty thousand die every day, appear before the tribunal of God's justice, and begin an eternity of either bliss or woe. Who can tell amongst this fearful number how many thousand there may be in a state of mortal sin? Pray for them: they are your brethren in Jesus Christ, perhaps even relatives, friends or benefactors. Pray for them, and pray especially for all sinners who are at the point of death. Time flies, tomorrow it will be too late. The day will come when you too will be in your agony, when you too will stand in need of prayers, and what a consolation will they not be to you in this your last and terrible struggle.

EXAMPLE

A young libertine, who had given himself up to every kind of disorder and crime, was dying of consumption, cursing his existence, and rejecting all thought of religion. His father who was still more deeply steeped in iniquity, endeavored to persuade him to commit suicide, in order to put an end to his sufferings, adding that he too would destroy himself and thus together they would escape the burden of life. A pious lady, terrified at the dispositions of the dying man, and horrified with the blasphemies of the unhappy father, hastened to recommend them to the prayers of the Archconfraternity of Our Lady of Victories. Many joined in supplicating and imploring her whom the Church calls the Hope of the despairing and the Patroness of a good death, to have pity on those miserable souls who were about to fall into eternal flames. The heart of Mary was moved, and she obtained from her Son the miracle which was asked of her.

During the two following days the young man still appeared melancholy and preoccupied, but at length he asked for a priest, made his confession, publicly acknowledged his crimes, and invoked with many tears the protection of the Blessed Virgin. "She has saved me," exclaimed he, "I shall die happy and contented." The next day was Saturday, and he asked for a rosary. His sister offered him her own. "Put it round my neck," he murmured, and laying his head on the pillow, he gently breathed his last.

The father wept over his son, and, conquered by grace, he in his turn was converted, and made a holy death, with his last breath publishing the mercies of God and the Blessed Virgin. These wretched men had intended to commit suicide; probably they had no mother on earth to comfort them, or to inspire them with better feelings, but their Mother in heaven obtained for them resignation and the grace of a happy death. How true is it that Mary is always the sure refuge of poor sinners.

PRAYER

O Mary! powerful Protectress of the dying, do not abandon us at that last hour which will decide our eternal lot. Be near to bless us, to comfort and defend us. Preserve us from a sudden and unprovided death, and obtain for us the grace of dying fortified by the last sacraments, pronouncing thy saving name. Amen.

TWENTY-FOURTH DAY

MARY, MOTHER OF THE SOULS IN PURGATORY

I. She consoles them.
II. She delivers them.

First Point.—Mary is not satisfied with consoling those among her children who yet tread the difficult path of life, or those who, having reached the end of their career, are preparing to cross the dread threshold of eternity. She is also the comforter of the souls who are detained in purgatory by the justice and the love of God. Where is the mother who would not rush to the rescue of her child if she saw it falling into a fiery furnace when it lay in her power to render it assistance? And will Mary, the most tender of Mothers, be indifferent to the torments of her children plunged in the expiatory flames of Divine Justice? Oh, no! Full of compassion for these suffering souls she is ceaselessly engaged in procuring them some alleviation. There is no pain in that dark prison which she does not soften; not one hour passes but she pours a cooling stream on that avenging fire. "Oh!" exclaims St. Vincent Ferrer, "how good is Mary to the poor prisoners who groan amidst the flames of purgatory! Not a moment passes but through her intercession they receive relief and aid." The Holy Virgin, speaking in revelation to St. Bridget said: "I am the Mother of all who are in purgatory, and the pains which are inflicted on souls, in order to expiate their sins, are lightened by my prayers." Happy, indeed, are the true Children of Mary; she not only protects them in this world, but extends her compassion to their unseen pains in purgatory, those pains beyond the tomb. Oh! what comfort should not this thought afford us.

Following the example of Mary, we too should strive to succor these unhappy victims of Divine Justice, for are they not our relatives, our benefactors, our friends? Perchance amongst them may be found a father, a mother, husband or wife, a brother or sister. Perhaps it is because they have loved us too well, that they suffer so cruelly and endure tortures like to those of hell, with the exception that they are not eternal. Their only resource is to borrow the voice of the Church and to say to us, "Have pity on me, have pity on me, at least you my friends, because the hand of the Lord hath touched me" (Job, 19:21). Let us compassionate and help these poor souls, and one day they also will take pity on us. "*Miseremini.*"

Second Point.—The Blessed Virgin does not limit herself to visiting and relieving the holy souls in purgatory, but by her intercession she obtains their deliverance. To hasten the termination of their sufferings, she inspires the living to help them by their prayers and good works, and supplicates her Divine Son to end their torments and admit them to the abode of refreshment, light, and peace. What Mary asks she always obtains. How many forgotten or insufficiently-aided souls would weep for ages in this place of unspeakable torments if the Blessed Virgin did not hasten the hour of their deliverance? How many, liberated through her maternal love, enter heaven on those days when the Church celebrates her touching festivals? The learned and pious Gerson assures us that on the day of her Assumption into heaven, all the souls who were then in purgatory were liberated by her intercession; and Denis the Carthusian adds: "That on several feasts of the year the Queen of Heaven descends into the abode of expiation to deliver

thence souls there detained, separated from God."
The Blessed Virgin, appearing to Pope John XXII,
spoke these words: "If among the religious and
associates of the Carmelite Order who leave this
world there are any whose sins deserve purgatory,
I their glorious Mother, will descend into their
midst the Saturday after their death, and I will take
them up into the holy mountain, into the happy
regions of eternal glory." Oh, how comforting it is
to think that if we fall into purgatory the merciful
Virgin will extend to us her hand to draw us out of
this fiery prison, and to place us near Him in
eternal bliss.

Children of Mary, we too should strive to
deliver souls from purgatory. We can do so, first,
by indulgences, that precious treasure formed by
the superabundant merits of Jesus Christ and the
saints; secondly, by our prayers recited with
attention and fervor, even if it were but the pious
aspiration, "Good Jesus, grant them eternal rest;"
thirdly, by alms, which deliver from all sin and
cover iniquities; fourthly, by Mass and
Communion. St. John Chrysostom saw in vision an
angel, who poured the Precious Blood from the
chalice into the abyss of purgatory, and the purified
souls winged their flight into heaven. Can charity
be said to reign in us, if with such easy means of

alleviating and delivering these poor souls, we neglect to do so? What injustice and what ingratitude should we not be guilty of?

EXAMPLE

A holy priest who had the affliction of losing a pious friend to whom he was devotedly attached, hastened to offer the Sacrifice of the Mass in honor of the Blessed Virgin for the repose of his soul. At the Memento for the Dead, with great recollection fixing his eyes on the Sacred Host, he said, "My God, behold the soul of Jesus Christ thy Son, that pure and perfect soul in whom Thou art well pleased. I offer it to Thee for the relief and deliverance of the soul of my friend. I ask, O Lord, a soul for a soul. For the sake of Thy Son here mystically immolated, and of Mary so intimately associated with his sacrifice on Calvary, O Lord God, save and deliver him whom I so tenderly loved, and for whom I shall never cease imploring thy mercy."

His prayer was heard. At the end of Mass, God permitted that the departed should appear to thank the priest, and to assure him that the Mass he had just celebrated in honor of the Blessed Virgin, had delivered him from purgatory. "After the Consecration," said he, "the Mother of God descended into purgatory, she broke my chains, and opened for me the gate of heaven. To you I owe my gratitude, to Mary I owe my love forever and ever." Oh, how many friends and departed brethren should we deliver from purgatory if we often heard Mass and received Communion for them. Most clement Virgin, teach us how to relieve the holy souls in purgatory.

PRAYER

O Mary, Star of Jacob, who shinest on that ocean of fire, which we call purgatory, have pity on those poor souls to whom thou art always the Mother and the Hope. Give ear to their sorrows, oh, thou who so often didst console them on earth. Jesus will be moved by thy prayers; heaven will open for them, and they will bless the Mother and the Son for all eternity. Amen.

TWENTY-FIFTH DAY

THE HOLY SCAPULAR

I. Its origin.
II. Its advantages.

First Point.—Consider, children of Mary, that of all the devotions to the Blessed Virgin, that of the scapular is the most esteemed, the easiest and the most secure. The origin dates from near the end of the thirteenth century, when the blessed Simon Stock, General of the Carmelites, implored the Queen of Heaven to bestow on his Order a special sign of her protection. After many years spent in the practice of prayer and penance, the Blessed Virgin appeared to him, surrounded by a multitude of angels, and holding in her hands the sacred badge of the scapular, which she presented to him, saying, "Receive, my beloved son, this scapular, which I bestow on the Order of the Carmelites, and on all the associates, as a pledge of my love and special protection. It is a sign of predestination, a safeguard in all danger, and whosoever dies wearing this habit shall not suffer the flames of hell." This heavenly apparition and these consoling words filled Simon Stock and all the children of Carmel with joy. Attracted by the promises of the Blessed Virgin, kings and people flocked from all parts to the Carmelite monastery to receive the holy scapular. Most of the sovereigns of Europe gloried in wearing the livery of the Mother of God. Twenty-five Popes, who succeeded to the chair of St. Peter, have recommended this devotion, and have enriched it with indulgences. The Feast of Our Lady of Mount Carmel has been fixed for the 16th of July, the day of the miraculous apparition.

Such is the origin of the scapular: it is a remembrance of our Mother and it comes from her own hand. Who is there amongst us who will not hasten to assume so honorable a livery? Thousands of the highest rank, persons from all grades of society have gloried in wearing it, and shall we be ashamed to follow their example? Let us wear our scapular with the respect and confidence which it merits. Let us wear it always, let us never cast it aside; a disarmed soldier is already half vanquished. What a misfortune if we were to die without this garment of salvation! When we visit the sick let us make known to them the devotion of the scapular, if they are not already invested with it; by so doing we shall draw down on them the protection of Mary, and shall secure for them victory over the enemy of their souls, who will redouble his efforts to drag them down to hell.

Second Point.—What are the advantages derived from wearing the scapular? They are valuable and numerous: first, it gives us a right to the privileges and favors of the Blessed Virgin, who, by this mark, recognizes us as her children, whereas without this livery, she could say to us like the bridegroom in the parable to the foolish virgins, "I know you not." "*Nescio vos.*" Next, it secures for us a great share in the prayers and spiritual works of all the members of the Order and Confraternity of the Carmelites, so numerous throughout the world. Besides this, the scapular, as its name denotes, is a garment or sort of breastplate against the enemies of our salvation—the world, the devil, and our own passions. How many young people have recoiled from sin at the sight of the likeness of Mary. How many sinners have regained confidence when pressing it to their breasts, How many hardened souls in their last agony has it not softened and saved from hell. In the temporal order of things the effects produced by wearing this holy garment are not less wonderful, for through the efficacy of the scapular how many incendiary fires have been extinguished; how many shipwrecks avoided; how many shots rendered harmless; how many swords been broken; how many sick cured, and even dead resuscitated. Finally, its benefits extend beyond the grave; the Blessed Virgin has promised those who have worn it with faith, fulfilling the conditions, that she would descend into Purgatory the Saturday after their death, to deliver them, and to open for them the gates of heaven.

Children of Mary, what a treasure do we not hold in our hands. Let us value fully a devotion so rich and so beneficial to those who deserve it. But let us not forget that to wear the livery of the Queen of Heaven is to bind ourselves to lead a pure life, to walk in her footsteps, and to be entirely devoted to her. In the words of the Church, this habit is holy, "Vestimenta hæc sancta sunt." Let us then wear it with joy and reverence, and let us rather die than desecrate it by mortal sin. "*Potius mori quam fædari.*"

EXAMPLE

Not many years ago, a young man living at Marseilles, a victim to his bad passions and the pleasures of the world, was on the point of death. He had forgotten God, he had given up everything, even his scapular, and he was dying in a state of frenzy and despair. His pious sister wept and prayed in vain for him, he resisted all her efforts and blasphemed though the shadows of death were falling on him. His poor sister perceived it, she hastened from the room weeping, but returned a few minutes later, holding in her hand her scapular, which she had taken off to give to her brother.

"Charles," said she, "you have no longer the scapular which our mother gave you on the day of your first Communion, and which you then were so glad to wear. Here, take mine with confidence as a remembrance of your sister; the Blessed Virgin will bless you," and whilst saying this, she passed it round his neck. Wonderful to relate, the sick man heaved a deep sigh, and fervently clasping it to his bosom, he called on the Blessed Virgin to come to his assistance. A priest being sent for, he administered to the dying man the last rites of the

Church, and a few hours later the gates of heaven opened to receive the child of Mary.

His sister, though she mourned his loss, derived comfort from the recollection of his happy death and the assurance she had that those who die clothed with the scapular will be preserved from eternal flames. "*In quo quis moriens non patietur incendium.*"

PRAYER

Holy Virgin, our Lady of Mount Carmel, I promise to wear your holy habit all the days of my life. I will clasp it to my heart in all my dangers and temptations, and it will prove my strength and salvation. By this sign recognize me at the hour of death as thy faithful servant, and place me near thee in heaven.

TWENTY-SIXTH DAY

THE DEVOTION OF THE ROSARY

I. A devotion illustrious in its origin.
II. A devotion holy in its object.

First Point—The institution of the Rosary in its present form is due to the illustrious St. Dominic, the founder of the Order of Friar Preachers, and who was one of the greatest servants of the Blessed Virgin. After having long and unsuccessfully preached against the errors of the Albigenses, who denied the virginity of Mary, and ravaged the south of France by their depredations, he retired to a chapel of Our Lady, near a solitary forest, where he passed three days in prayer, beseeching with tears the help and assistance of the Queen of Heaven, against the enemies of religion and the country. It was then that the Mother of Mercy appeared to him, resplendent with majesty, and herself revealed to him the devotion of the Rosary. "Know, O my son," said she, "that the means that the Adorable Trinity made use of to announce salvation to the world was the Angelic Salutation. If, therefore, you desire to conquer these hardened hearts, preach the devotion of my Rosary, you shall obtain from it the happiest results." St. Dominic at once became the apostle of the Rosary; he taught the people the spirit of the devotion and the method of reciting it, and the effect produced by his sermons was soon marvelous. In a short time one hundred thousand heretics were brought back to the bosom of the Church, a multitude of sinners were converted, and the moral aspect of a part of France and Spain was changed. From that moment this admirable devotion spread with rapidity, produced everywhere the most abundant fruit, and is at the present time the favorite practice of all true children of Mary.

Let us always carry our Rosary about us, as the insignia of the servants of the Queen of Heaven, and as a safeguard in the perils which surround our innocence; let us carry it with reverence uninfluenced by human respect. Let us say it often, at least in part, either kneeling before a picture or statue of the Blessed Virgin, in our leisure moments, or on our way to our work. Those who never fail saying the Rosary every day cannot be lost, for it unites them to Mary as with a chain, and each Hail Mary is like a precious pearl which is added to her eternal crown. Blessed Alain did not hesitate to declare that devotion to the holy Rosary is a mark of predestination.

Second Point.—The devotion of the Rosary merits our love and respect. To glorify Jesus Christ, to honor the Mother of God, to sanctify our own souls, such is its object, such is the threefold end which every servant of Mary should have in view. Moreover, the prayers which compose it, being the Lord's prayer and the Angelic Salutation, there can be none more holy in themselves and more agreeable to Jesus and Mary. The meditation of the different mysteries recalls to our memory the virtues and examples of our Savior and his holy Mother. Lastly, the fruit of holiness that this admirable devotion has produced in souls are immense. No person who has been in the habit of reciting the Rosary has failed to experience its salutary effects. Thus the Church has enriched it with the treasure of its graces, and heaven has testified to it by striking miracles. Oh! how holy, venerable, and precious, is this devotion, and how dear it should be to us.

Consider, children of Mary, that there are many ways of saying the Rosary well: the first is to attend to the sense of the words you pronounce and let the meaning sink into your hearts. The second manner is to reflect on the different mysteries of the Rosary, which, each in its turn, was a subject of joy, of sorrow, and of glory to Jesus and Mary. In these grand mysteries which sum up the life of our Savior and our Mother, is there not abundant matter for meditation? The third manner is to propose to ourselves at each decade, some one particular intention, which, engaging the understanding and the heart, prevents weariness and distractions; for instance, the conversion of a sinner, the recovery of a sick person, or the deliverance of a soul from purgatory. Have we hitherto had recourse to these different means of saying the Rosary well?

EXAMPLE

A convict at Toulon, having stabbed his keeper, was condemned to death, and the execution was to take place two days after the sentence. The chaplain visited the condemned man several times, offering him the consolations of religion, but his offers were refused, and the convict, heaping insults on him, uttered the most horrible blasphemies. To enforce silence, he was chained and gagged; there was no time to lose, the fatal hour was at hand, and the scaffold was being erected. Profiting by the restrained position of the prisoner, the chaplain threw his Rosary round his neck, recommending him to the Blessed Virgin. Oh! how merciful is Mary to sinners; no sooner had the Rosary touched him than he became calm, relented, and with tears asked to make his confession. He was happily reconciled to God before appearing at the tribunal of Divine Justice, and he asked pardon of all whom he had scandalized. This furious man had become gentle as a lamb. The keepers who assisted at his execution were astonished to find him so quiet and so resigned, and could not help rendering their homage to the Mother of God, who had transformed an abominable wretch into a holy penitent.

PRAYER

We give thee thanks, O Mary, for having given us the holy Rosary, a chain of love, composed of fifteen golden links, which unite us more Closely to thy heart and to that of thy Son. To show our gratitude, we promise that we will profit by so precious a gift, often and devoutly reciting it. Oh! may this Rosary which we shall frequently bear in our hands, be the pledge of the crown which thou wilt one day place on our brows.

TWENTY-SEVENTH DAY

THE ANGELICAL SALUTATION

I. The prayer the most pleasing to Mary.
II. The most efficacious prayer, next to the Lord's prayer.

First Point.—To recall to the humble Virgin of Nazareth, that memorable day, when the archangel Gabriel came to announce to her glad tidings; when the Eternal Word took flesh in her chaste womb, and without ceasing to be God, became her Son; to proclaim her full of grace, in her conception, in her birth, and in her whole life; finally, to resume in a few words all the hymns of Sion, all the panegyrics of the holy doctors of the Church, all the prayers of fervent souls, is this not rendering to Mary a homage worthy of the Queen of Heaven, worthy of the Mother of God? When, according to a pious author, she heard for the first time this salutation from the mouth of the archangel she conceived in her most pure womb the Word of God; and each time that a human mouth repeats this Ave, which was the sign of her maternity, her soul is moved, her heart is gladdened and all the assembly of the saints rejoice at the happiness which she feels. The Blessed Virgin revealed to St. Mechtilda, that of all prayers this one was the most pleasing to her, and blessed Alain said, "that the words Ave Maria fill heaven with joy, and the demon with fear."

Children of Mary, you recite daily and many times a day the Angelic Salutation, but do you pay attention to its meaning, so glorious to the Blessed Virgin and so consoling to you? Do you sometimes meditate, one by one, these inspired words, and seek to relish with heart and mind the hidden manna which they contain. Doubtless this beautiful prayer becomes dull and wearisome when recited through custom, without reflecting on the sublime meaning to which it gives expression; but when it is said with attention and devotion it is always found to be more and more touching and beautiful. For the future make it an occasional subject of meditation at the foot of the altar, so that when you say it, it may always be with the respect it merits, and the attention it requires. Remember the often-repeated words of the learned Suarez, "I would give all my writings for one Ave Maria well said."

Second Point.—According to St. Bernard, each time that we salute Mary by this prayer we are saluted by her in return. This great saint having one day pronounced these words, "*Hail Mary*," heard this consoling answer, "I too, Bernard, I hail thee." "The salutation of the Mother of God," adds St. Bonaventure, "consists always in some precious grace which she bestows on those who honor her." We continually find in the lives of the saints, innumerable instances of protection, which prove the power of this prayer over the heart of our beloved Mother. How beautiful when lisped by the innocent child, Mary listens to, and blesses it. How beautiful on the lips of the orphan, Mary adopts him and becomes his mother. How beautiful when uttered by the sinner, inspired by hope and repentance, for Mary will then obtain mercy and pardon. How beautiful when breathed by the sick and the dying, Mary will come to their assistance and lead them to heaven. Indifferent Christians and infidels have been met with, who no longer remember the Lord's Prayer, but very rarely is one to be found who has forgotten the *Ave Maria.* Happy are those who recite it daily, for there is hope that the merciful Virgin will not allow them to perish, and that at least, at the hour of death, she will remember to pray for them.

Children of Mary, the Angelic Salutation will be for you a source of grace and benediction, if you frequently recite it with confidence. Let us then resolve to say it at least morning, noon, and night. Many persons repeat it each time the clock strikes the hours. The holy Curé D'Ars established in his parish the excellent custom of sanctifying every hour by the repetition of the *Ave Maria*. Whether in the pulpit, or in society, he never failed when the clock struck to pause and offer this homage to Mary; let us all, after his example, do in like manner.

EXAMPLE

A few years ago a little book of Catholic prayers fell by chance into the hands of a young English Protestant, fourteen years of age. She opened it, and her eyes fell on the *Ave Maria*, which was unknown to her. She perused it a second time more slowly, and said to herself, "that she had never read anything so beautiful and so consoling." This sublime salutation touched her heart and inspired her with a profound respect and great love for the Blessed Virgin, whom Protestants disown and insult. She learned the *Ave* by heart, repeated it often and frequently, spoke of it to her parents and friends. She was at first laughed at, then censured, and finally was ill-treated. The poor child suffered all without complaining, and continued to recite the prayer, which inspired her with a secret dislike to Protestantism and a great love for the Catholic Church. In the meantime her brother died, and her mother taking her to France, her first care was to place herself under instructions, and shortly afterwards she abjured heresy and had the happiness of being received into the true Church. From that day she never omitted saying her favorite prayer to obtain from the Blessed Virgin her mother's conversion. Her desires were speedily realized, the mother followed her daughter's example, and the two were never weary of reciting the Angelic Salutation, to which they owed their salvation.

PRAYER

O Holy Virgin Mary, blessed amongst women, beloved of the Lord, pray for thy poor children; be with us now, for at every hour we need thy heart and hand to support and comfort us. But above all, be with us at the hour of our death. As thou wert our first friend, be thou our last, and at that dread hour receive our trembling soul and plead for it with thy Son, our Sovereign Judge. Amen

TWENTY-EIGHTH DAY

THE "MEMORARE"

I. The excellence of this prayer.
II. Its efficacy.

First Point.—It is well known that the *Memorare* is one of the best prayers that can be addressed to the Blessed Virgin. It was composed by the seraphic St. Bernard, and contains in an eminent degree the two essential conditions for prayer—confidence and humility. After recalling the evidence of centuries, the devout St. Bernard reminds Mary that never was it known in any age, or in any place, that any of her servants, however miserable, however guilty they might be, had ever been abandoned. Always has she listened to the prayer of the unhappy, always has she responded to the cry of her children. "Behold me a poor sinner, unworthy, more unworthy than all others; behold me trembling at thy feet, "*coram te gemens peccator assisto.*" I am guilty, I ask for pardon; I am unhappy, I ask for pity; I am forlorn, I weep and I hope. Oh! by thy twofold title of Mother of God, and my

Mother, do not reject the prayers and the tears of thy child: "*Noli verba mea despicere.*" Could the Queen of Heaven, the Queen of Mercy, repel a soul which, humbling itself thus at her feet, confides and gives itself to her without reserve? Will not such confidence, such loving trust, secure for us her maternal protection? Will not humility and confidence, such as this, draw down on us a flood of mercy?

Children of Mary, it is in this way that the illustrious St. Bernard loved to pray to the Queen of Heaven, and it is thus that we too should love each day to pray. But are we animated with the same feelings, the same interior dispositions? Instead of our hearts being gladdened with feelings of confidence and love when we utter the words, "Remember O most Holy Virgin," are they not weighed down by earthly affections? Instead of being truly humble and contrite at the recollection of our countless sins, are we not full of self-esteem and attachment to creatures? O most clement Virgin, forget our unworthiness, and remember only thy mercy: *audi, benigna, et exaudi.*

Second Point.—This short and simple prayer is nevertheless very efficacious, and the compassionate heart of Mary is never closed against it. It has drawn down from heaven a thousand times more graces than it contains letters, and innumerable miracles have been obtained by saying it with confidence. It has been called by some the miraculous prayer, and truly so, for how many just souls has it not encouraged and sustained in the battle of life? How many sinful souls have regained their confidence in Mary when saying, "Remember, O most holy Virgin Mary, that thou hast never been invoked in vain." How often has a criminal, hitherto impenitent, shed tears repeating these sweet words, and how many hardened sinners, at the hour of death, has not a Memorare softened and saved from hell? In the seventeenth' century, a holy priest called Bernard worked many miraculous conversions by simply reciting the Memorare for sinners, and sometimes forcing them to say it with him. Yes, thousands of times has this cry of hope, the Memorare touched the heart of Mary; she has answered the urgent appeal, and has brought the lost sheep back to the fold, the prodigal to his Father's house, and the dying man on the verge of falling into eternal fire "How true is it," says a saint, "that heaven and earth will pass away sooner than Mary cease to succor those who confide in her and implore her protection."

Children of Mary, you too will obtain abundant aid if you frequently and piously recite this truly miraculous prayer. Resolve to repeat it at least once a day before an image of the Queen of Heaven, consider what grace you desire most for yourself or others, and ask it from your heart. Pray with humility and confidence, and you are certain to be heard.

EXAMPLE

One day a priest received a visit from a young man of most pleasing appearance, who said, Reverend Father will you be so good as to go at once to such a street, such a number, on such a floor, someone there stands in need of your spiritual assistance." The priest went at once to the house named, entered, and found a poor dying woman, abandoned by all. "I have come," said he, "as you sent for me." "I," replied the woman, "I never sent for you." "How is that," said the priest, "did you not send a son, a relation, or acquaintance?" "Certainly not," said she, "I am alone here, and in any case should never have went for a Catholic priest, for I am a Lutheran."

Astonished at this reply, and thinking who the messenger could possibly be who had sent him to the woman, it occurred to him to ask her if she had shared the dislike of her co-religionists towards the Blessed Virgin, or if she had ever honored and prayed to her? "Yes, sir," she answered, "I have invoked her daily, never have I forgotten to say a Memorare, and I have had only Mary to comfort me during my illness." "Doubtless," said the servant of God, "it is the Blessed Virgin, who, touched by your prayer, has sent me to you; she will not allow you to die in heresy. Do you not wish to embrace the true faith?" The heart of the poor woman opened to the appeal of grace; she renounced heresy, received all the sacraments, and died in the bosom of the Church. The priest was convinced that Mary had sent him the guardian angel of this chosen son to reconcile it with her Divine Son. Oh! how wonderful is the power of the Memorare.

PRAYER

Virgin most clement, source of all graces, how true it is that thou hast never been invoked in vain. Listen always favorably to the prayers of poor sinners, hearken graciously to us when prostrate at thy feet, and groaning under the weight of our crimes, we address to thee that beautiful prayer, "Remember, O most Holy Virgin." Oh, yes, remember always that thou art our Mother, and we thy children. Amen.

TWENTY-NINTH DAY

NOVENAS

I. How efficacious they are.
II. In what way they must be made.

First Point.—Consider that of all the exercises Of piety by which the Blessed Virgin is honored and invoked, one of the most efficacious and one of those most authorised by the Church is without doubt that of Novenas. It is the powerful means which the children of Mary make use of in all important and difficult matters to obtain extraordinary graces and great miracles, and few days pass, on which the faithful of all ages and all conditions are not seen prostrate at the feet of this powerful protectress to implore her aid by a Novena. The graces we ask for with confidence, Mary always obtains, or gives others more suitable for our needs and more useful for our sanctification. Many miracles prove that the Queen of Heaven cannot refuse to listen to these pious exercises. If, according to the testimony of St. Bernard, she hears a simple and hastily recited prayer, would she reject those that are during nine days offered to her with so much fervor and perseverance. Oh! no, it is impossible; for our Mother is too good. Let no one speak of thy love, O holy Virgin, who says that thou art ever invoked in vain. How often have we not heard it said, "I stood in need of an extraordinary grace, of an almost miraculous favor; I had recourse to Mary with confidence, I made a Novena in her honor, together with my friends and relatives, and at the conclusion I received what I had asked for." Assuredly, then, a Novena finds always acceptance with the heart of Mary our Mother.

Children of Mary, when you desire to obtain a signal grace, for example, the choice of a state of life, the deliverance from suffering, the cure of an invalid, the conversion of a sinner, preservation from pestilence, or a holy death, make with confidence a Novena of prayers in honor of the Blessed Virgin, and your request will certainly be granted. Do not in future neglect so useful a means of salvation, and recommend your friends and acquaintances to adopt the same course. Make also a Novena in preparation for each feast of the Blessed Virgin, such should always be the practice of those who are devoted children of Mary.

Second Point.—Be careful when making Novenas to do so with a very pure intention; have always in view the glory of God and the salvation of your soul. You must first of all be in a state of grace and renounce all affection to sin, for who can hope that the most pure and holy Virgin will bestow her favors on a soul the slave of passion and the friend of the devil. Be very exact and faithful to the different exercises and prayers appointed for these nine days, without however allowing them to interfere with the duties of your state of life, and invite your friends and relatives to unite their prayers to yours. If you are able, assist at Mass during the time of the Novena, and at its conclusion receive Communion; on the other days make a spiritual Communion. Practice greater recollection and closer union with God and the Blessed Virgin, and finally give an alms, if in your power. Thus, children of Mary, you will induce the Mother of God to obtain for you the object of your desires. Never forget to return thanks to your benefactress, for gratitude is a duty and claim to new favors. Oh! what ineffable joys, what signal graces are in store for you, if you often and piously make Novenas in honor of Mary.

EXAMPLE

A young woman, twenty-eight years of age, suffered for many years most acute pains. No remedy could be found to relieve her, and the physicians declared that she was incurable.

Her confessor finding her one day weeping and discouraged, endeavored to comfort her by saying that the Blessed Virgin, who is called Health of the Sick, would obtain her some relief. "O Father," said she, "for a long time I have been praying to the Blessed Virgin, but she has not heard me; my sufferings increase, I shall soon die." "Be comforted my child," he replied, "we will today begin a Novena for you, and a Novena well made Mary always hears favorably, as I have myself frequently experienced. This is what we must do. You and all the members of your family must go to confession, and on the first and last day of the Novena receive Holy Communion; secondly, your mother must each day say the Rosary and Litany of the Blessed Virgin by jour bedside; she must say all these prayers slowly so that you also may repeat them with devotion; thirdly, during the course of the novena you must unite your intention with mine during the Holy Sacrifice of the Mass. Courage then my dear child: your cure is certain if you are careful to observe these pious practices." The Novena began on the 17th of May, and on the last day the girl, waking from a deep slumber, cried out, "Mother, mother, come here, I am cured." Her relatives ran to her and found her cured, really and truly cured. Tears of joy filled the eyes of her mother, and all her family and friends returned thanks to God and to Mary for so great a favor. The next day the young girl went to the church and received Communion with her father and mother, and all the witnesses of the miracle chanted the Te Deum in thanksgiving.

PRAYER

Remember O most holy Virgin, that thou art our refuge in our perils, our consolation in our sufferings, and our resource in all our needs. Receive our supplications, and obtain for us the graces which we solicit through thy intercession, and which we expect with the firmest confidence. Amen.

THIRTIETH DAY

THE MIRACULOUS MEDAL

I. Miraculous in its origin.
II. Miraculous in its effects.

First Point.—In the year 1830, when the Revolution had broken out, and France seemed doomed to perish in the blood of her children, and religion was threatened with annihilation, a Sister of Charity of St. Vincent of Paul was praying and weeping before the a liar of the Blessed Virgin, when suddenly Mary appeared to her, resplendent in beauty, and in the attitude represented on the miraculous medal. A rich crown of stars encircled her head, and her arms were extended towards the earth, figured by a globe under her feet. From her hands fell rays of dazzling light, of which the most beautiful and numerous were directed to a particular point of the globe, indicating France. The vision seemed sent for two objects, to show how greatly France stood un need of the graces of divine mercy, and that these graces would be given through the hands of Mary. The humble daughter of charity, Catherine

Labouré, whose name until lately was concealed, revealed hex secret to her confessor, and he made it known to Monseigneur de Quélen, the then Archbishop of Paris, who ordered a medal to be struck depicting this vision, which was called the miraculous medal, and the devotion to it spread rapidly. At the present time it is to be found everywhere, in all countries, in all houses, and on all breasts. It is placed in the cradle of infants, on the bed of the sick, and it finds a resting-place on the heart of the brave soldiers as they march to battle. Doubtless the Immaculate Virgin wished, through the agency of this miraculous medal, to prepare our souls for the proclamation of the dogma of the Immaculate Conception, and for her later beautiful apparition at Lourdes.

Children of Mary, never be without one of these medals, it is worthy of your esteem, reverence, and confidence. Wear it always about you, it will be a sign of your filial devotion towards the Queen of Heaven, and a pledge of her maternal tenderness. The sight of this blest image speaking to your heart, will reanimate your fervor, and your love; and Mary will protect you in life and in death.

Second Point.—There is about this medal something still more miraculous than its origin, and that is its effects on souls and bodies. The number of sinners which through its means the Blessed Virgin has brought to repentance, the sick she has prepared fora good death, the weak she has comforted and cured, is countless. How often have sinners been converted by friends concealing medals about their persons. Others have consented to wear it near their hearts, and being spiritually enlightened, have sought and obtained pardon. Some who only kissed this little medal have been instantly converted, and have since persevered. It is related that a priest in Paris makes great use of the medal which has been the means, he says, "of obtaining the conversion of many souls." In speaking of the most hardened sinner, who, nevertheless, has accepted a medal, he says with the greatest confidence, "He is saved, his conversion is secured," and wonderful to relate, the effect speedily follows. These miracles have sometimes taken place without either the sinners or the sick having prayed, sometimes even without knowing they were prayed for by others, but the medal had been sewn to their clothes or placed in their pillows. They were saved through the faith of the person who had recourse to this pious stratagem.

Children of Mary, give this medal to the poor, to the sick, and to sinful souls, make them promise to wear it, and to recite the little prayer, "O Mary, conceived without sin, pray for us who have recourse to thee." Do this and you will save them, you will be exercising a true apostleship, you will cause the Queen of Heaven, your Mother, to be known and loved, and you will draw down on yourself and on all those you love eternal blessings and mercies.

EXAMPLE

A pious person was very intimate with a young lady, a neighbor of hers, who lived a worldly life and had given up the practice of her religious duties. One day she said to her, "I have just received some very beautiful medals, will you accept one?" "What should I do with it," answered the friend; "I should not dare wear it, and moreover do not care about it." "But I beg of you all the same to take one, and if you will not wear it out of devotion to the Blessed Virgin, keep it at any rate as a remembrance of my friendship; it cannot do you any barm, on the contrary, it may do you a great deal of good." "The lady could not refuse so earnest a request and she accepted the medal. A few days later she returned to her friend and said,

"Since I have begun to wear your medal, my mind is much disturbed and troubled with thoughts urging me to be converted, I feel God is moving me by his grace. Take me to your confessor; I wish to give up the world and its pleasures and to think seriously about the salvation of my soul." She made her confession, received Communion, and her happiness was so great that she cried for joy when thanking her friend for the service she had rendered her, and kissing the medal, she promised to wear it respectfully till death.

PRAYER

We resolve, O tender Mother, to wear thy miraculous medal with respect, piety, and confidence. Often will we press it to our heart and lips, and every where it shall accompany us. May it be our shield in all dangers of soul and body, in life and in death. Amen.

THIRTY-FIRST DAY

PERSEVERANCE

I. It is a duty.
II. It is a necessity.

First Point.—Children of Mary, we have now reached the last day of this month of graces and benedictions. It is the solemn hour for our last prayer. Alas! it is also the hour to bid farewell to this beautiful season. Say, what return will you make to Mary for all the graces she has bestowed upon you during these thirty days? Recall to your minds these daily gatherings around her altar; those united supplications addressed to her with so much fervor; those pious exhortations that told of her love and tenderness for us; those sacred hymns and harmonious canticles. Finally, let all examine their own souls, and number, if they can, all the graces and gifts that they have received from their tender Mother during the days of this festive month—graces of conversion, graces of perseverance and fervor, graces for themselves and their brethren, for the living and the dead, graces for this present life, and for the dread hour of death. Know that the least of these numberless graces is worth more than the whole world. Recall also to your minds all that you have felt and experienced that was great, virtuous, and heavenly in the course of this month; see what Mary has done for you, and what have you done for her? What return will vou make to her for so many benefits? "Quid retribuam?" Will you not promise to love her always, and to persevere till death in her service? Gratitude obliges you to this; it tells you, that if you forget Mary, after having experienced for a whole month so many consolations and so much happiness, you would be guilty of the greatest ingratitude. No, indeed, you will never forget her, you will invoke and bless so tender, so generous, and so loving a Mother.

O Mary! O my good Mother! may my right hand wither, may my tongue remain without life, may I die at your feet, if my heart should cease to love thee.

Second Point.—Consider, in the second place, that we ought to persevere in our devotion to Mary, because to-morrow as well as today: next month, as well as this, we shall need her help and maternal protection: "Just as a body," said St. Philip, "cannot live without breathing, so a soul cannot live without devotion to the Mother of God, by which is obtained and preserved in us the life of grace." Perseverance is necessary, because in attaching ourselves irrevocably to the service of Mary, we shall be enabled to conquer all the enemies of our salvation. In the language of Scripture, is she not strong and powerful as an army in battle array. Yes, we must persevere, because devotion to Mary is a sign of predestination: "Holy Virgin," exclaims St. Alphonsus Liguori, "if I persevere in loving, serving, and invoking thee, my crown is secured." Let us then persevere, for we have only a little time on earth in which to love our tender Mother: life is short, death approaches with rapid strides. Happy, a thousand times happy, shall we be if we can live and die in the arms of Mary our Mother.

The following are a few means which will help you, children of Mary, to persevere each day, morning and night, you must address a fervent prayer to Mary: for instance, the Hail Mary, the Memorare, or a part of the Rosary. In whatever state you find yourself, even should you have fallen into mortal sin, you must not abandon this pious practice, it will bring you happiness.

Each week, on Saturday, assist devoutly at Mass, in honor of the Blessed Virgin, it is a counsel recommended in many pious books. Saturday may be called the Sunday of the Mother of God: a day et grace and benedictions for all her children.

Each month, frequent the sacraments of Penance and Holy Eucharist, and unless one of the great solemnities of the Church occur, prefer to approach on a feast of the Blessed Virgin. She will herself present you to her Divine Son, and Jesus, for his Mother's sake, will shower his blessings on you. Thus, under the protection of this glorious Queen, days, weeks, and months will pass peacefully, until we return to celebrate once more, with renewed fervor, this beautiful month, or if death comes to close our eves, Mary will open for us the gate of heaven, where we shall bless her forever.

EXAMPLE

St. Edmund of Canterbury, having reached the age of manhood, resolved to consecrate himself to God by a vow of perpetual chastity. But in so important an affair, the young student determined to seek counsel from an experienced guide. "If you wish," said his saintly director, "to overcome all attacks of temptation, and preserve a conscience without stain, consecrate yourself to the Mother of Mercy, and bind yourself to her by an eternal engagement. Your perseverance in her love and service will be a pledge of your innocence and salvation." Edmund, on receiving this advice, went to the altar of the Queen of Virgins, placed at the feet of her statue two rings, around which he had caused to be engraved the Hail Mary, and kneeling down pronounced a vow of perpetual chastity. He then took one of the rings and placed it on the finger of the holy image, as a pledge of his vow and inviolable alliance; the second he kept for himself, and placed it on his own finger... This ring was from henceforth sacred in the eyes of the young man; he wished to keep it till death, as a sign of his indissoluble union with the Queen of Virgins. Raised later to the See of Canterbury, he would have no other Pontifical ring, and after his decease it still remained on his hand. What an example of perseverance is not this for us, children of Mary: imitate this youthful saint, and consecrate yourself entirely and forever to your Mother. Act of Consecration to the Blessed Virgin.

O beloved Mother and all-powerful Sovereign, at the conclusion of this blessed month, which has seen us united each day at the foot of thy altar, receive the solemn consecration that we make to thee of our hearts and souls, of all that we are, and of our entire lives. We know that in thy maternal heart there is a place for each and all of thy children, that thy goodness extends to all our miseries, and thy graces equal our needs. Yes, O Mary, we are thine, we belong to thee, as children belong to their mother; accept, then, the homage of our love, confidence, and devotedness. Tor ever, yes, forever, we will belong to thee, and we will bless thee; never permit us to be unfaithful to thee.

PRAYER

O great and tender Mother, love us and bless us a, love and bless those whom we love, and whom we would fain name here prostrate before thee, Love and bless our country, our beloved Pontiff, and our Mother, the one, holy, Catholic Church, enlighten the blind, calm the angry passions of men, and give us peace. Be to us, O merciful Virgin, the gate of heaven, so that one day we may be all united around thy throne of glory, as we now are at the foot of thy altar, to bless and love thee for all eternity. Amen.

PRAYERS FOR ASSISTING AT MASS IN UNION WITH MARY

Preparation.

God of power and majesty, with the help of thy grace, I am about to assist at the most august and sacred of the mysteries of our holy religion. I desire to profit by the favors which Thou dost abundantly vouchsafe to those who come animated with an ardent desire of Thy divine love. Fill my soul with this same spirit of charity, of self-sacrifice, and of abnegation with which the heart of Mary was penetrated at the foot of the cross. May the dispositions of thy Blessed Mother be also mine. I cannot present to Thee a pure soul like hers, nor the abundance of her virtues, but I offer Thee a heart desirous to obey Thy holy law, to profit by the shedding of Thy Precious Blood, and the outpouring of Thy love, so that I may become more virtuous. O my God, grant that this august sacrifice at which I am about to assist may conduce to the salvation of my soul. Holy Virgin, help me to put aside all distractions which might prevent my deriving the full benefit of the Mass which I am about to hear.

At the Confiteor.

I confess to Almighty God, to blessed Mary ever Virgin, to blessed Michael the Archangel, to blessed John the Baptist, to the holy apostles Peter and Paul, and to all the saints, that I have sinned exceedingly in thought, word, and deed: through my fault, through my fault, through my most grievous fault. Therefore I beseech the blessed Mary ever Virgin, blessed Michael the Archangel, blessed. John the Baptist, the holy apostles Peter and Paul, and all the saints, to pray to the Lord our God for me. Amen.

At the Kyrie Eleison.

Have mercy on me, O my God, pardon the number and enormity of my sins, which deserve indeed Thy anger, but listen to my supplications; have pity on me, and purify my soul. Powerful Queen of Heaven, thou art the refuge of sinners; I am one of the most guilty. I implore thy help to avert the justice of God, whose vengeance my sins have deserved.

Aft the Gloria in Excelsis.

I will praise Thee, O God, and bless, adore, and give Thee unceasing thanks here on earth, hoping one day to continue the same eternally in heaven. Almighty Being, Thou alone art all great and all powerful, receive the homage I desire to offer Thee, in union with that which Thy most holy Mother rendered Thee during the course of her life; hear my prayers, and blot out my iniquities.

At the Collects.

Lord, we unite our supplications to those of the priest, Thy minister; grant us the assistance that he asks for the salvation of our souls and our temporal needs. Fill us with Thy love, and grant us the grace to be always faithful to Thee; we ask this through the intercession of thy holy Mother.

At the Epistle.

Divine Jesus, make my understanding attentive and my heart docile to the sacred truths announced to us by the prophets and apostles; do not permit that they should serve to my condemnation, but grant me grace to listen and profit by them. Inspire me with sentiments of piety and fervor, like those with which thy holy Mother was penetrated, when she listened to the words of life which issued from Thy sacred lips.

At the Gospel.

Imprint, O Lord, in my heart the laws of the Gospel, grant that my conduct may be ever regulated by them alone. Inspire me with contempt for the maxims of the world, which would only cause the loss of my soul, and I will neither follow nor listen to them. Give me grace to imitate Thy glorious Mother, who kept in her heart the remembrance of Thy words and actions.

At the Credo.

My God, I believe without doubting all the truths contained in the Apostles' Creed, and I will live and die in this faith. Grant that my belief may be animated by good works. Holy Virgin, thou wast declared blessed, because thy faith was a living and active one; it has merited for thee the favors which heaven showered down on thee; obtain for me the grace to be submissive and faithful to whatever is taught and ordained by the Catholic Church.

At the Offertory.

Divine Savior, I offer Thee all I have and am; from Thee I have received all, to Thee I desire to sacrifice all when Thou demandest it of me. Receive this offering in union with that which the Blessed Virgin made to Thee.

At the Lavabo.

Cleanse my soul, O my God, efface all the stains which disfigure it in Thine eyes; restore to it the beauty it received in baptism, and which it has lost by sin. Immaculate Virgin, thou wert exempt from all stain. I am sinful, and have long been in this state, obtain for me the grace never more to offend God.

At the Orate Fratres.

Divine Jesus, give me love of prayer and the grace to pray well; penetrate me with the recollection and fervor which I should have when assisting at this sacrifice, which the priest offers to Thee for the glory of Thy name, the salvation of souls, and the benefit of the whole Church. Holy Virgin, intercede for me, so that thy adorable Son may grant my petitions.

At the Preface.

My heart shall no longer be engrossed with earthly things, to Thee alone, O my God, do I consecrate it. I unite myself with all the heavenly court to render Thee my homage, and to thank Thee more worthily for all the gifts of nature and grace, which Thy divine mercy has vouchsafed to me. Blessed Virgin, thou art our advocate in heaven, offer to God my prayers so that they may be pleasing in His sight.

At the Sanctus.

O my God, how holy Thou art, and how sinful am I! Thy sanctity raises Thee infinitely above us, but Thy love brings Thee down to sanctify us. Holy Virgin thou didst co-operate in our salvation by becoming the Mother of our Divine Redeemer; help me to bless Him, to glorify and thank Him for all He has done for me.

At the beginning of the Canon

All powerful God, Father of mercies, we most

humbly implore Thee to accept the sacrifice we offer thee; grant that we may receive the full benefit of it. Most august Mother of our loving Savior, beg Him to bestow His blessing on our sovereign pontiff, on our bishop, and all the faithful.

At the Memento for the Living.

Lord Jesus, listen to the prayers of those who assist at this holy sacrifice. I recommend to Thee my parents, my benefactors, my friends, and enemies. I ask for them and for myself all those graces which Thou knowest to be needful for our salvation, deign to grant them through the merits of the glorious Virgin Mary and of all the saints whom we invoke.

At the Elevation of the Host.

O sacred Body of Jesus, I adore Thee, present in the consecrated Host. Eternal Father, it is Thy Divine Son who takes upon Himself to be our victim for Thy glory and our salvation; I unite my homage to that which He pays Thee, Holy Virgin, from thee our Redeemer has received the adorable body immolated for us on the cross and on our altars; most holy Mother of God, obtain for us the graces which are the fruits of this sacrifice.

At the Elevation of the Chalice.

My loving Savior, it is Thy sacred Blood, it is Thy divine person that I adore in this Chalice. Holy Virgin, this Precious Blood has flowed in Thy pure veins, ask of thy Divine Son to apply its merits to me, to purify and sanctify my soul.

At the continuation of the Canon.

O Lord, do not permit Thy servants to be unmindful of what Thou hast done and suffered for them; the holy sacrifice of the Mass recalls daily the remembrance of Thy benefits, may we receive its salutary effects; this is the grace we ask, through the intercession of Thy Blessed Mother.

Memento of the Dead.

Cast down, I implore Thee, O God, a look of pity on the poor souls who suffer in the flames of purgatory, and speedily receive them into the abode of peace and glory. Listen to their sighs, and grant them the eternal glory which Thou hast destined for them. Queen of Heaven, Mother of Mercy, we beg thy help for these suffering souls.

At the Pater Noster.

Our Father, who art in heaven, hallowed be Thy name, Thy kingdom come, thy will be done on earth as it is in heaven. Give us this day our daily bread, and forgive us our trespasses as we forgive them that trespass against us; and lead us not into temptation, but deliver us from evil. Amen

At the Libera nos.

Lord, deliver us from our sins, grant us the grace no longer to commit them, and preserve us from the eternal pains we have deserved. Remove from us the occasion of displeasing Thee, and all that could disturb the peace of our souls. Holy Virgin, protect us, not only against the enemies of our salvation, but in all the dangers with which we are threatened.

At the Agnus Dei.

Divine Lamb, adorable Victim, who wast immolated for us, Thy Blood has effaced our sins;

perfect the purification of our souls, have mercy on us, make us worthy of receiving peace, which is one of the fruits of thy Sacrifice. Mother of God, pray to thy beloved Son, that his merits may be applied to us.

At the Communion.

O Divine Jesus, how happy are Thy ministers and the faithful, whom Thou dost permit to receive Thee every day in Holy Communion. Oh, if I had but the same happiness, the same dispositions. Lord, I acknowledge my unworthiness, which deprives me of so great a blessing; Thou alone canst satisfy the desires of my heart. The little zeal I bring to receive the Bread of Life causes the dryness I complain of; make me, then, more worthy to approach Thy Sacred Table. Most pure Virgin, obtain for me the grace not to depart this world without being strengthened by the Holy Viaticum.

At the Last Prayers.

I give Thee thanks, O my God, for having allowed me to participate in Thy Sacred Mysteries; grant that I may carefully preserve the remembrance and the fruits of them. I ask it through the merits of Jesus Christ, who has offered and immolated Himself in this august Sacrifice, at which I have had the happiness of assisting in honor of the glorious Virgin Mary, the Queen of men and angels.

At the Blessing.

O all-powerful God, Father, Son, and Holy Spirit, give me Thy blessing, so that, assisted by Thy grace, I may be always faithful to Thy commandments. Holy Virgin, the Lord has poured on thee the abundance of his benedictions; intercede for me, so that I may have the happiness of participating in them.

At the Last Gospel.

Eternal Word, who didst become man to make us the children of God, I thank Thee for this ineffable grace, and for having deigned to dwell amongst us. Render me grateful for the honor Thou hast done me in adopting me for Thy child; grant that my life may be worthy of this inestimable character, so that I may be of the number of those blessed ones of Thy Father, and that I may reign with them in the kingdom of thy glory. O purest of virgins, it was in thy sacred womb that the Son of God became incarnate; this title of Mother of our adorable Savior makes thee, after the most Holy Trinity, the most worthy object of our love and confidence, Receive the homage we offer thee and grant us thy protection.

Prayer after Mass.

I beg pardon, O my God, for the wanderings of my thoughts, and the coldness of my heart, when I ought to have been wholly occupied with Thee, and inflamed with Thy love. I thank Thee for the favor Thou hast done me, and I will now go with confidence wherever Thy holy will calls me. I will during the day remember this great grace, and I will endeavor, neither by word, action, nor desire to render myself unworthy of Thy blessing.

Holy Virgin, thou wilt aid me during this day to practice the good resolutions I have made during this Holy Sacrifice, and which ought to contribute to my sanctification.

Daily Prayers to the Blessed Virgin for each Day of this Month

Ave Maria

Ave Maria, gratia plena, Dominus tecum. Benedicta tu in mulieribus, et benedictus fructus ventris tui, Jesus. Sancta Maria, Mater Dei, ora pro nobis peccatoribus, nunc et in hora mortis nostrae. Amen.

Hail Mary, full of grace, the Lord is with thee. Blessed art thou amongst women, and blessed is the fruit of thy womb, Jesus. Holy Mary, Mother of God, pray for us sinners, now and at the hour of our death. Amen.

Memorare

Memorare, O piisima Virgo Maria, non esse auditum a saeculo, quemquam ad tua currentem praesidia, tua implorantem auxilia, tua petentem suffragia, esse

Remember, O most gracious Virgin Mary, that never was it known that anyone who fled to thy protection, implored thy help, or sought thy intercession was left derelictum. Ego tali animatus confidentia, ad te, Virgo Virginum, Mater, curro, ad te venio, coram te gemens peccator assisto. Noli, Mater Verbi, verba mea despicere; sed audi propitia et exaudi. Amen.

unaided. Inspired with this confidence, I fly to thee, O Virgin of virgins, my Mother; to thee do I come; before thee I stand, sinful and sorrowful. O Mother of the Word Incarnate, despise not my petitions, but in thy mercy hear and answer me. Amen.

Sub Tuum Praesidium

Sub tuum praesidium confugimus, Sancta Dei Genetrix. Nostras deprecationes ne despicias in necessitatibus, sed a periculis cunctis libera nos semper, Virgo gloriosa et benedicta. Amen.

We fly to thy patronage, O holy Mother of God; despise not our petitions in our necessities, but deliver us always from all dangers, O glorious and blessed Virgin. Amen.

Regina Coeli

Regina caeli, laetare,
alleluia:
Quia quem meruisti
portare, alleluia,
Resurrexit sicut dixit,
alleluia.
Ora pro nobis Deum,
alleluia.

O Queen of heaven
rejoice! alleluia:
For He whom thou didst
merit to bear, alleluia,
Hath arisen as he said,
alleluia.
Pray for us to God,
alleluia.

Mary, Mother of Grace

Maria Mater gratiae,
Mater misericordiae,
tu me ab hoste protege
et hora mortis suscipe.

Amen.

Mary Mother of Grace,
Mother of mercy,
Shield me from the
enemy
And receive me at the
hour of my death.

Amen.